Get Ready For
Kindergarten

★ LETTERS & SIGHT WORDS ★

Handwriting

Spelling

Proper Names

Phonics

Word Searches

Heather Stella

More than **Stickers**

BLACK DOG
& LEVENTHAL
PUBLISHERS

ISBN: 978-1-57912-937-8

Library of Congress Cataloging-in-Publication Data on file
at the offices of Black Dog & Leventhal Publishers, Inc.

Manufactured in the United States

Published by
Black Dog & Leventhal Publishers, Inc.
151 West 19th Street
New York, New York 10011

Distributed by
Workman Publishing Company
225 Varick Street
New York, New York 10014

h g f e d c b a

Contents

Letters: A, B, C	4	Words: WILL & NOW	66
Words: AM & WITH	6	Letters: J, K, L	68
My World: Birthday	8	Words: PRETTY & SAW	70
Letters: D, E, F	10	Letters: M, N, O, P	72
Words: BUT & DID	12	Words: WHO & SOON	74
My World: Family	14	Letters: Q, R, S	76
Letters: G, H, I	16	Words: TOO & UNDER	78
Words: GET & GOOD	18	My World: Reduce, Reuse, Recycle	80
My World: Food	20	Letters: T, U, V	82
Letters: J, K, L	22	Words: YES & NO	84
Words: MUST & NEW	24	Letters: W, X, Y, Z	86
My World: Community	26	My World: All about Me	88
Letters: M, N, O, P	28	Letters: A, B, C	90
Words: OUT & PLEASE	30	Words: EAT & WENT	92
My World: Neighborhood	32	My World: Family	94
Letters: Q, R, S	34	Letters: D, E, F	96
Words: SAY & SHE	36	Words: INTO & LIKE	98
My World: Animals	38	My World: Exercise	100
Letters: T, U, V	40	Letters: G, H, I	102
Words: THEY & THIS	42	Words: ON & OUR	104
My World: Reduce, Reuse, Recycle	44	Letters: J, K, L	106
Letters: W, X, Y, Z	46	Words: RIDE & RAN	108
Words: ARE & AT	48	Letters: M, N, O, P	110
My World: All About Me	50	Words: THAT & THERE	112
Letters: A, B, C	52	My World: Animals	114
Words: CAME & DO	54	Letters: Q, R, S	116
My World: Family	56	Words: WANT & WAS	118
Letters: D, E, F	58	Letters: T, U, V	120
Words: HAVE & HE	60	My World: Neighborhood	122
My World: Food	62	Letters: W, X, Y, Z	124
Letters: G, H, I	64	Answer Key	126

Aa Bb Cc

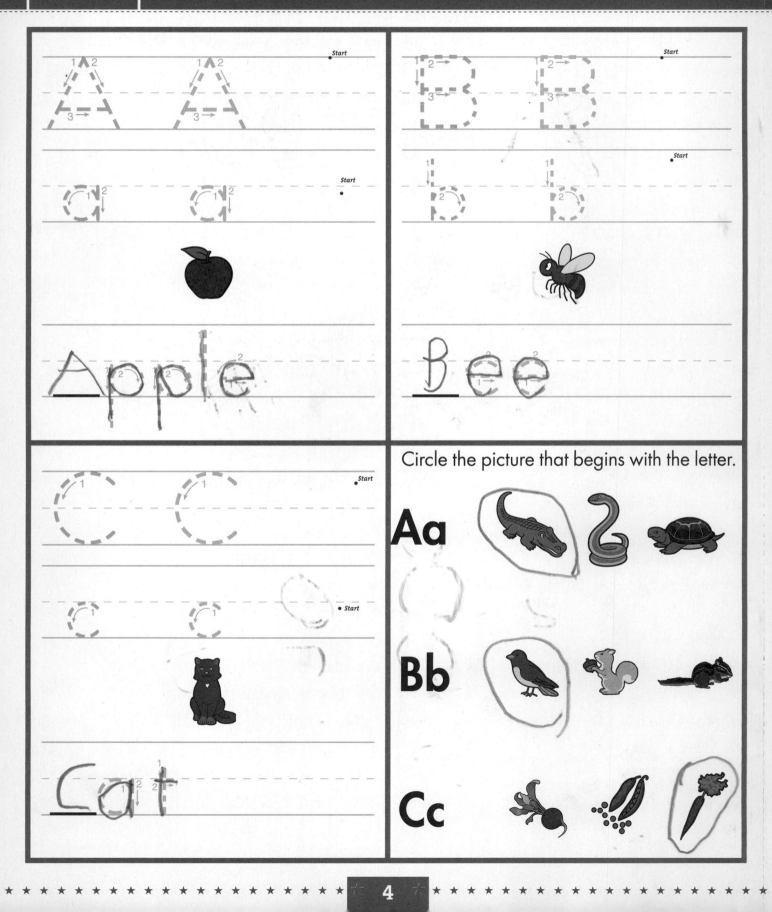

Apple

Bee

Cat

Circle the picture that begins with the letter.

Aa

Bb

Cc

Color in the spaces with the letter **A orange**, **B red**, and **C black**
to see what insect begins with the letter **B**.

Circle the letters in each row that match the first letter.

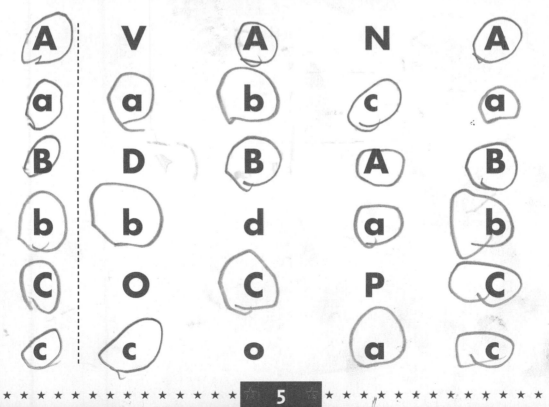

Trace the sight word on the dotted lines. Write it to complete the sentence.

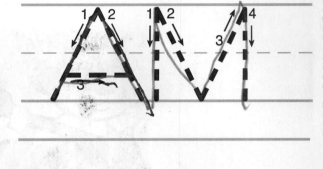

I __AM__ 6 years old today!

am   am   am

Color the boxes with the word **am**.

am	in	are
all	am	at
is	as	am

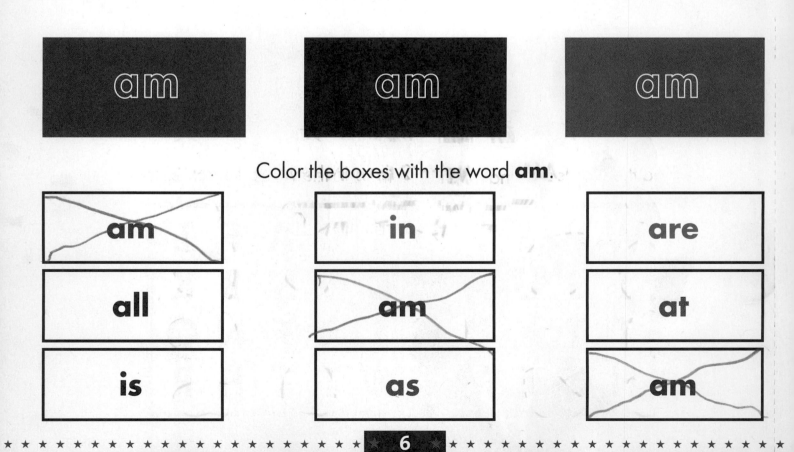

Trace the sight word on the dotted lines. Write it to complete the sentence.

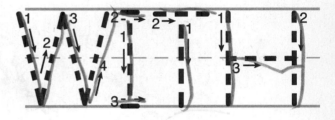

I like the clown ___with___ the red nose.

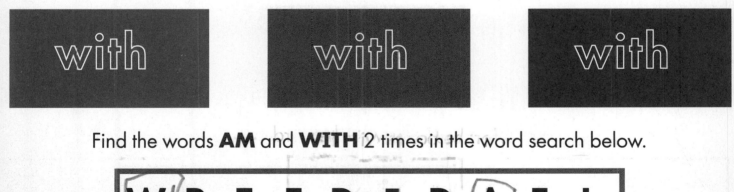

with   with   with

Find the words **AM** and **WITH** 2 times in the word search below.

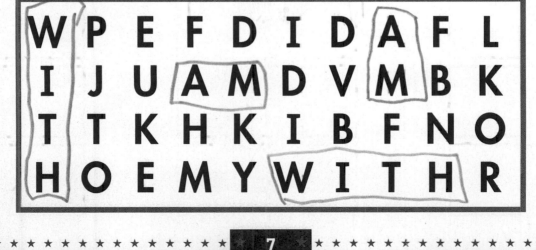

W	P	E	F	D	I	D	A	F	L
I	J	U	A	M	D	V	M	B	K
T	T	K	H	K	I	B	F	N	O
H	O	E	M	Y	W	I	T	H	R

When is Your Birthday?

Circle the month and day of your birthday.

My birthday is

January **February** **March** **April** **May**

June **July** **August** **September** **October**

November **December**

1 2 3 4 5 6 7 8 9 10 11 12 13

14 15 16 17 18 19 20 21 22 23 24

25 26 27 28 29 30 31

Draw candles on the top of the cake—one for each year of your age.
Now you decorate your cake!

Birthday Party Word Search

Done!

Find and circle the birthday party words from the word box in the word search below.
The words may be up, down, or across.

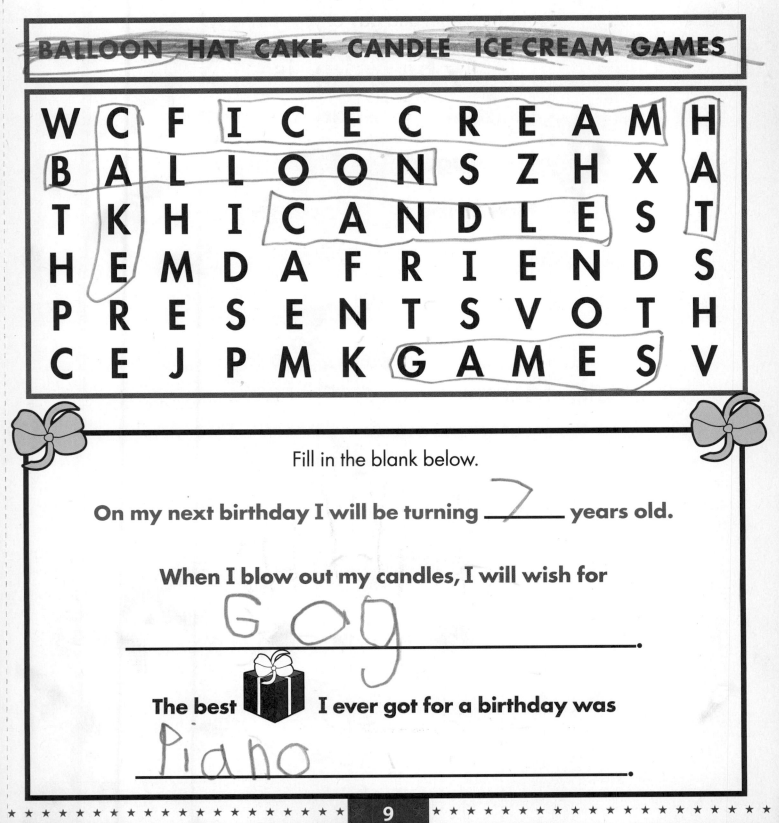

BALLOON   HAT   CAKE   CANDLE   ICE CREAM   GAMES

W C F I C E C R E A M H
B A L L O O N S Z H X A
T K H I C A N D L E S T
H E M D A F R I E N D S
P R E S E N T S V O T H
C E J P M K G A M E S V

Fill in the blank below.

On my next birthday I will be turning ___7___ years old.

When I blow out my candles, I will wish for

_G o g_____.

The best 🎁 I ever got for a birthday was

_Piano_____.

Done!

Dd Ee Ff

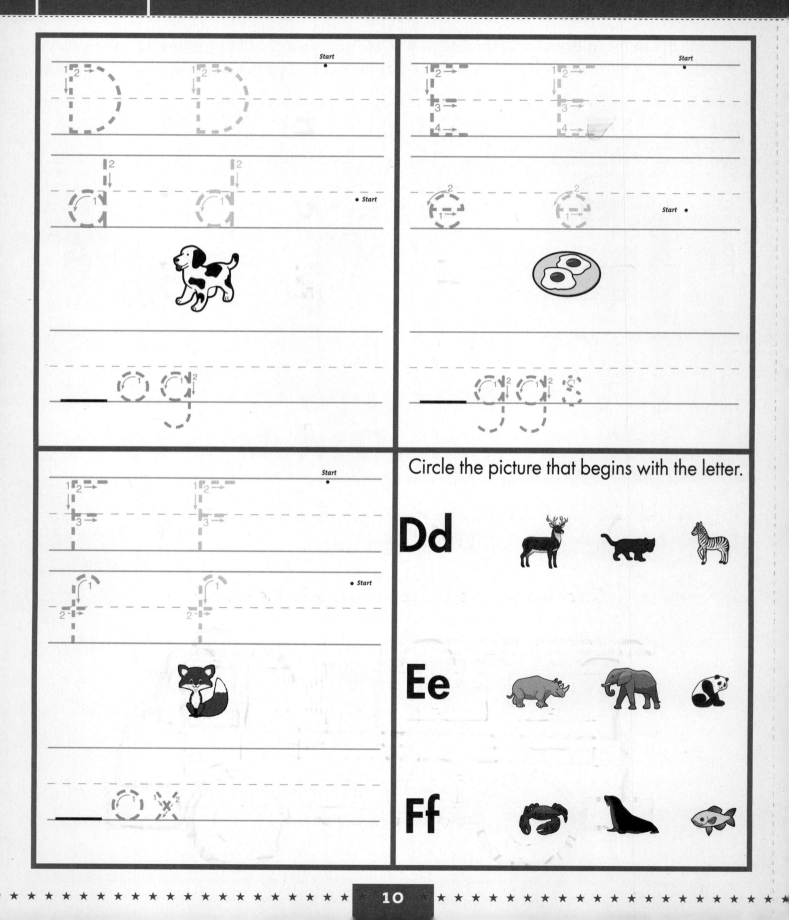

Circle the picture that begins with the letter.

Dd

Ee

Ff

Circle the letter in each row that is the beginning sound of the picture to the left.

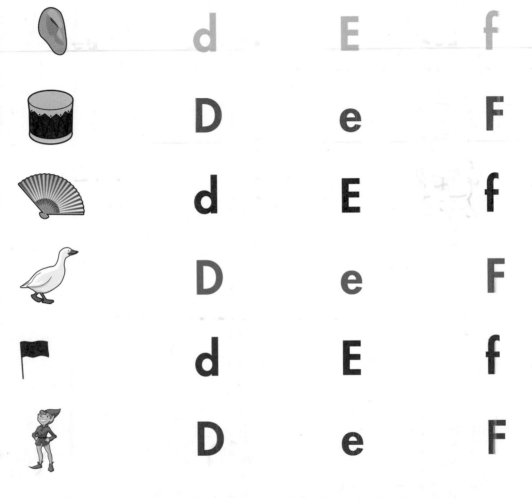

d   E   f

D   e   F

d   E   f

D   e   F

d   E   f

D   e   F

Color the fire truck, which begins with the letter **F**.

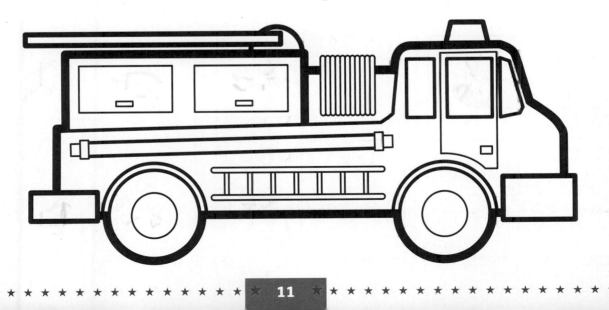

Done!

BUT

Look at the sight word. Trace it on the dotted lines and then try writing it yourself.

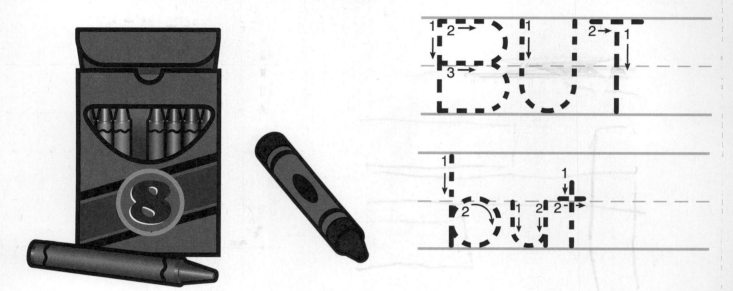

I like blue _____ my favorite color is red.

| but | but | but |

Color the boxes with the word **but**.

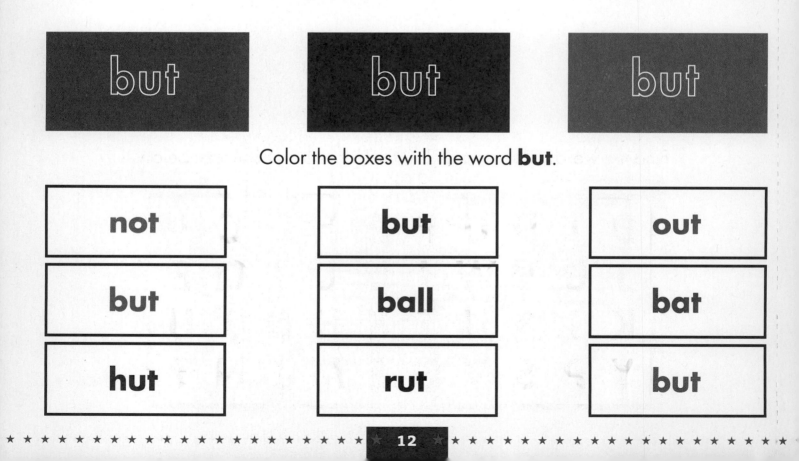

not	but	out
but	ball	bat
hut	rut	but

DID

Look at the sight word and trace it on the dotted lines. Then try writing it yourself.

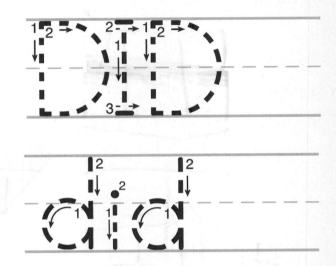

D_____ you have a good time at the zoo?

did　　did　　did

Find the words **BUT** and **DID** 2 times in the word search below.

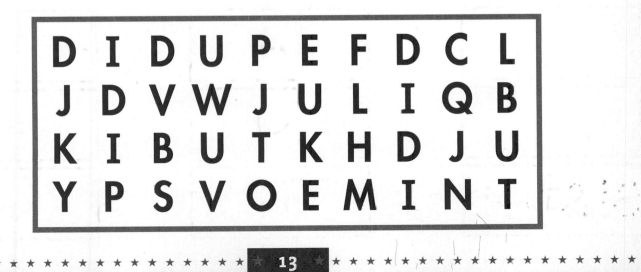

D	I	D	U	P	E	F	D	C	L
J	D	V	W	J	U	L	I	Q	B
K	I	B	U	T	K	H	D	J	U
Y	P	S	V	O	E	M	I	N	T

Done!

Family Members

Trace the names of family members below.

grandpa

mom

brother

dad

grandma

sister

My Family

How many people are in your family?

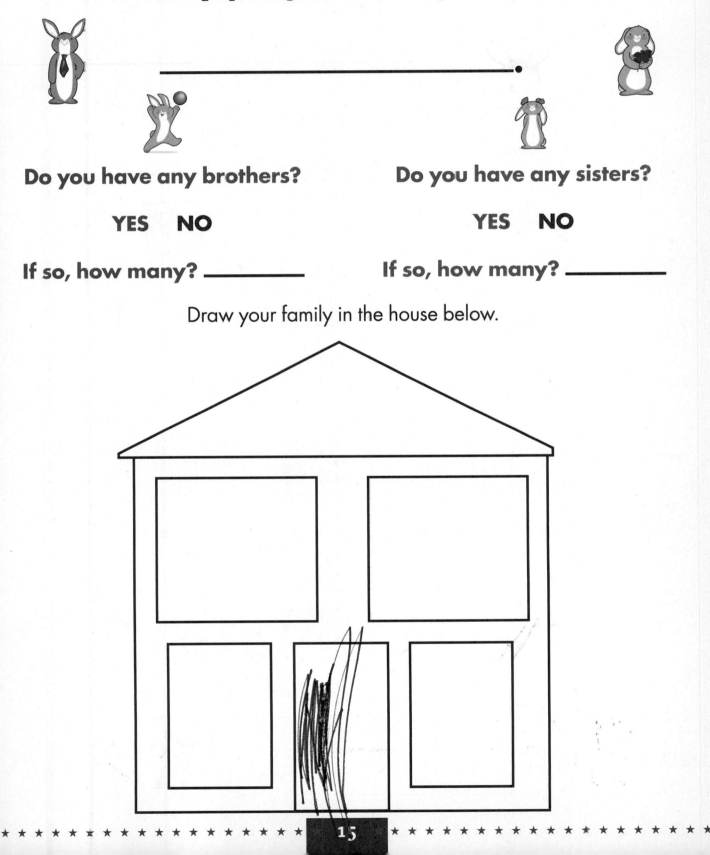

_____

Do you have any brothers?

YES   NO

If so, how many? _____

Do you have any sisters?

YES   NO

If so, how many? _____

Draw your family in the house below.

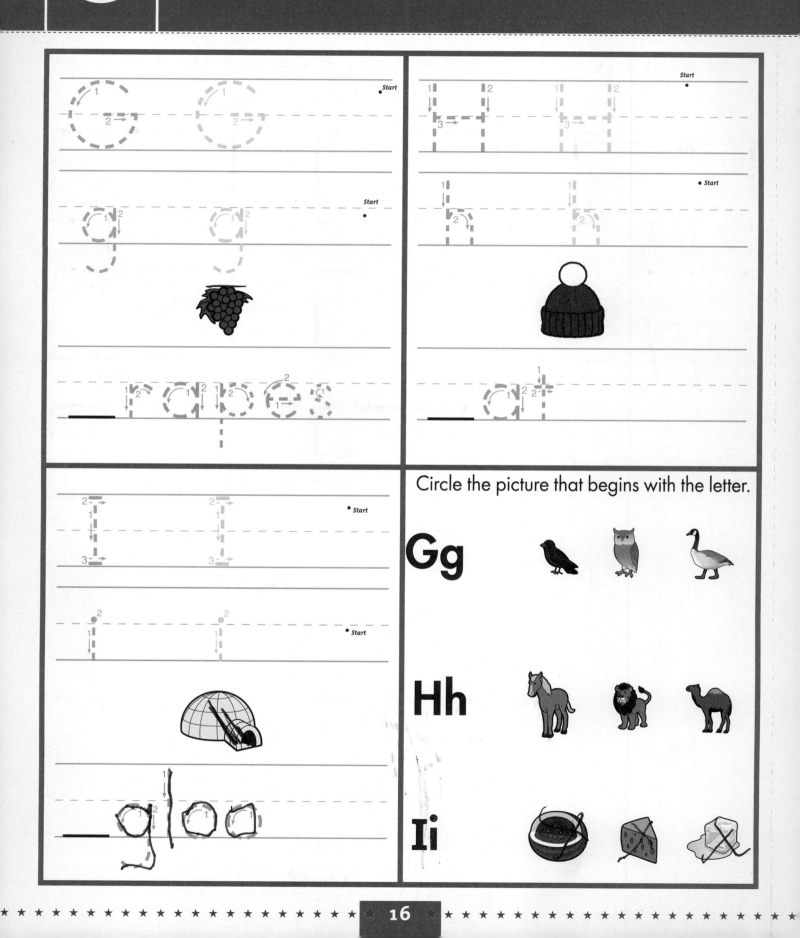

Circle the picture that begins with the letter.

Gg

Hh

Ii

Gg Hh Ii

Trace the letters up to **G**, **H**, **I**.

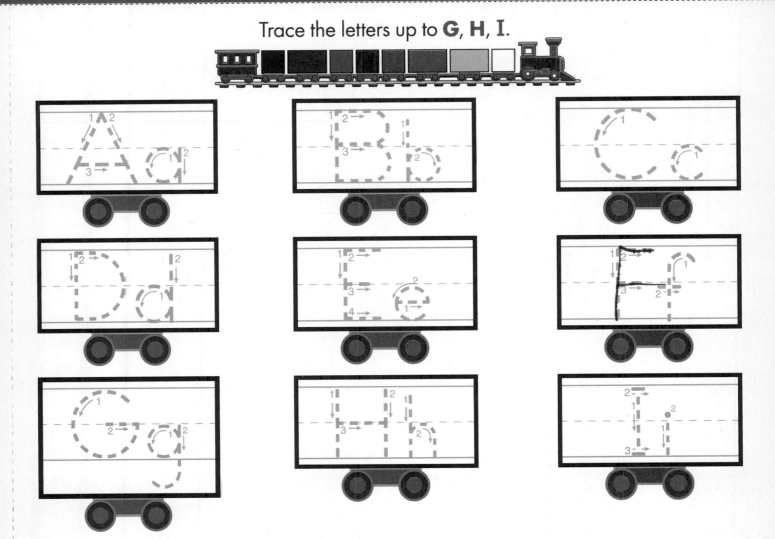

Color all of the **G's red**, the **H's green**, and the **I's orange**.

Done!

GET

Trace the sight word on the dotted lines. Write it to complete the sentence.

Please, can we _____ a puppy?

get	get	get

Color the boxes with the word **get**.

go	bet	get
got	get	set
met	got	get

GOOD

Trace the sight word on the dotted lines. Write it to complete the sentence.

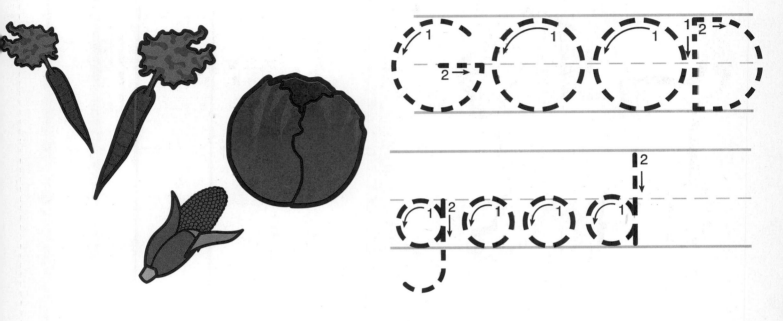

Vegetables are _____ for you!

good · good · good

Find the words **GET** and **GOOD** 2 times in the word search below.

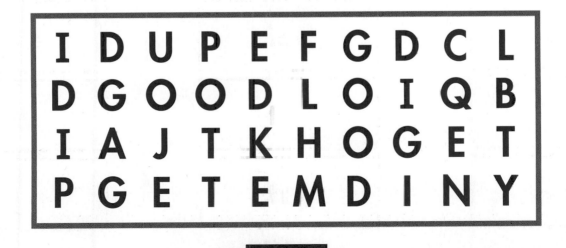

```
I  D  U  P  E  F  G  D  C  L
D  G  O  O  D  L  O  I  Q  B
I  A  J  T  K  H  O  G  E  T
P  G  E  T  E  M  D  I  N  Y
```

Done!

The Food Pyramid Plate

Eating healthy foods not only keeps your body strong but it gives you more energy to play. Below is a picture of the **food pyramid plate**.

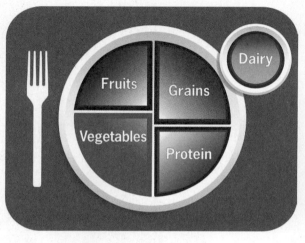

Circle the unhealthy foods that you shouldn't eat often.

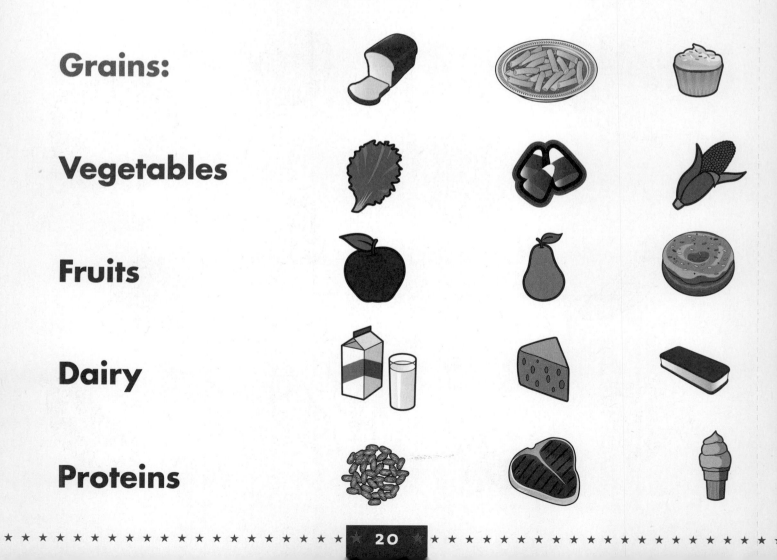

Grains:

Vegetables

Fruits

Dairy

Proteins

Fruits and Vegetables

Fruits and **vegetables** can add a rainbow of color to your meal,
plus they keep you healthy!

Draw a **square** around all the **vegetables**.
Draw a **circle** around all the **fruits**.

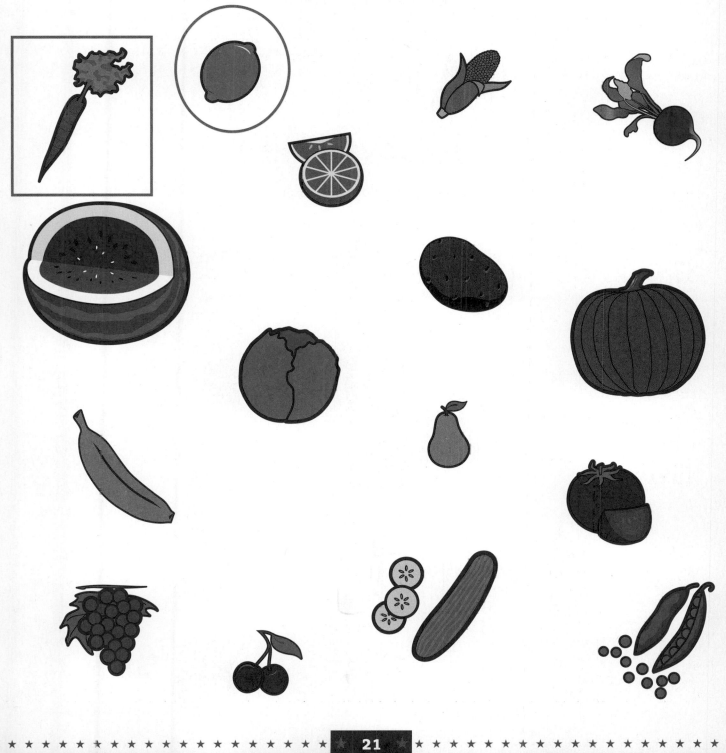

Jj Kk Ll

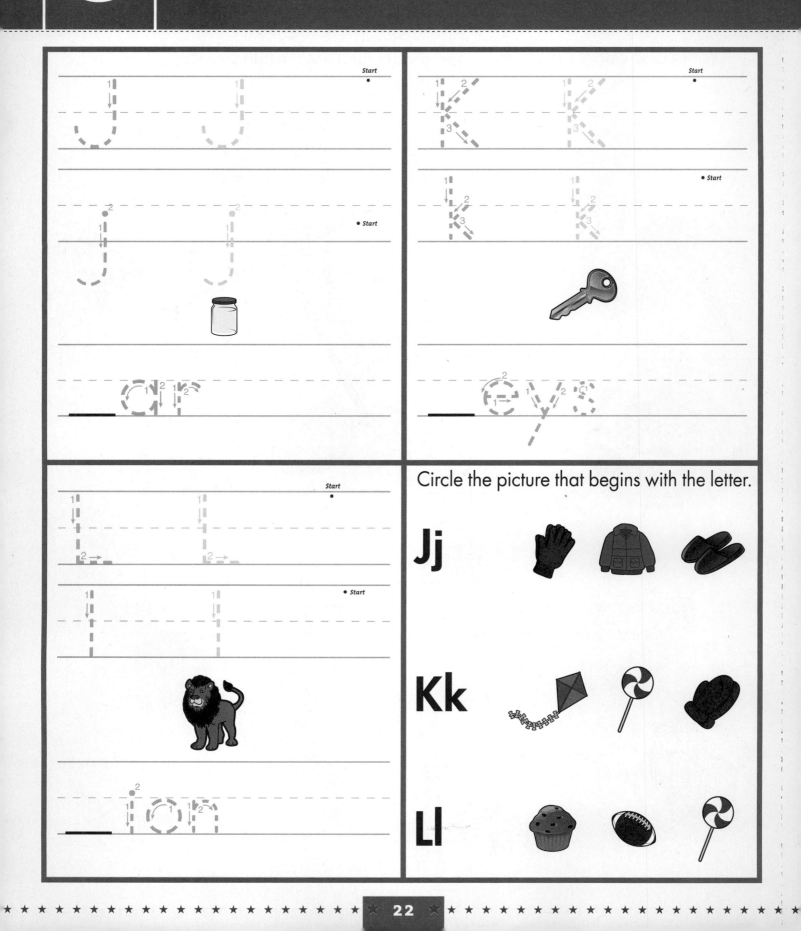

Circle the picture that begins with the letter.

Jj

Kk

Ll

Jj Kk Ll

Done!

Connect the dots **A** through **L** in order to reveal the hidden picture. Color it in.

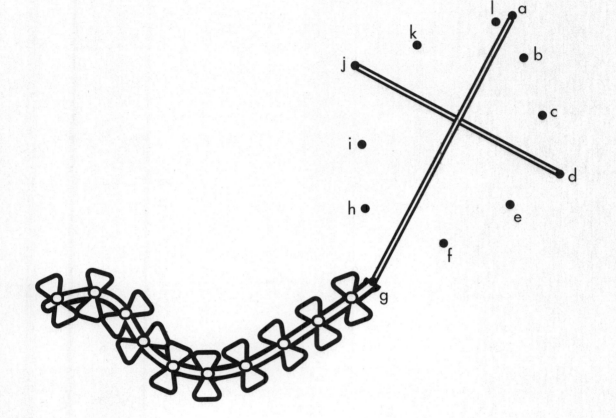

Trace the word and then say it out loud. Listen to the sound **Ll** makes.
Now draw something that starts with the sound **Ll** makes.

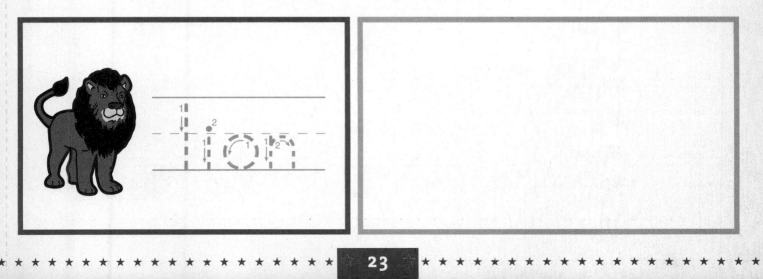

Done!

MUST

Trace the sight word on the dotted lines. Write it to complete the sentence.

You _____ practice your letters every day.

must   must   must

Color the boxes with the word **must**.

mom	must	most
must	more	much
might	dust	must

NEW

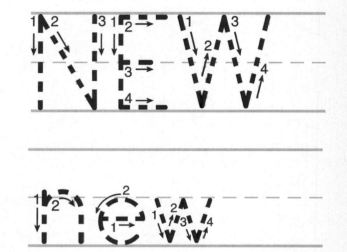

Done!

Trace the sight word on the dotted lines. Write it to complete the sentence.

I got a _____ bike for my birthday.

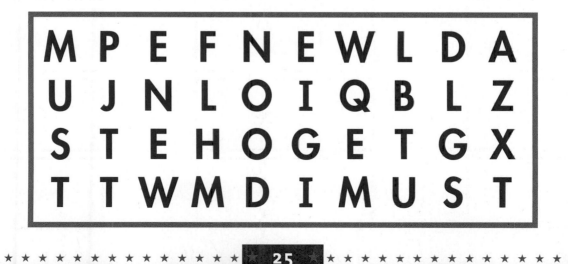

new   new   new

Find the words **MUST** and **NEW** 2 times in the word search below.

M	P	E	F	N	E	W	L	D	A
U	J	N	L	O	I	Q	B	L	Z
S	T	E	H	O	G	E	T	G	X
T	T	W	M	D	I	M	U	S	T

Done!

My Community

A **community** is where people live and work together.

People either live in a city, a town, or in the country.

What type of **community** do you live in?

City   Town   Country

All **communities** have a police station. Can you draw a picture of a police station?

How is your Community Special?

Done!

What does your **community** look like? Circle the things below that you can find in your **community**.

Houses

Railroads

Forests

Buses

Playgrounds

Horses

Street Signs

Taxis

Tall Buildings

Ponds

Mailboxes

Farms

Big Trucks

Boats

Zoo

Beach

Igloo

Bike Riders

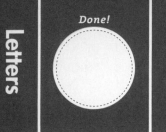

Done!

Mm Nn Oo Pp

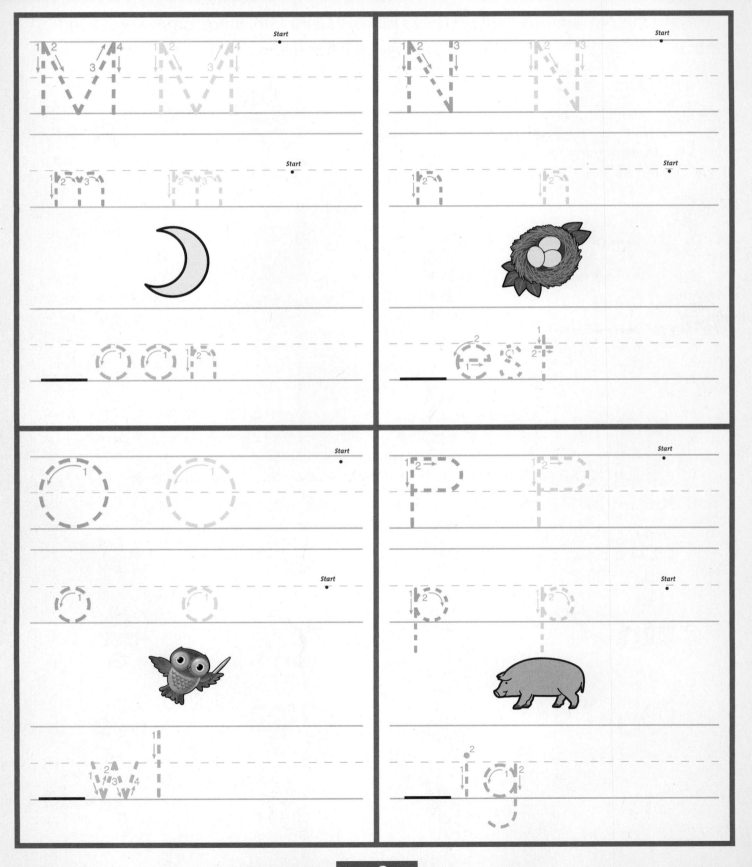

Look at the picture and then write the missing letter that is the beginning sound.
Then draw a line to that letter.

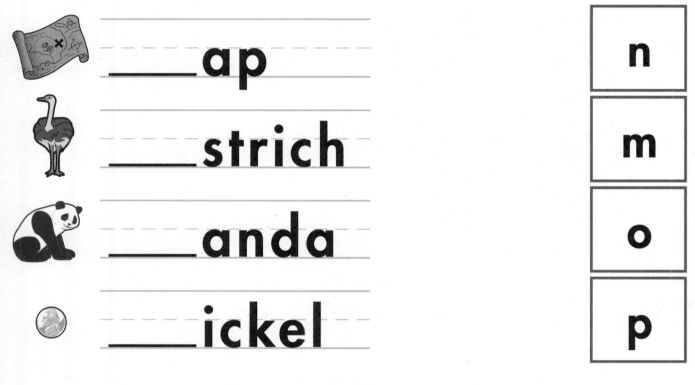

_____ap

_____strich

_____anda

_____ickel

n

m

o

p

Circle the picture that begins with the sound the letter makes.

Mm

Nn

Oo

Pp

Done!

OUT

Trace the sight word on the dotted lines. Write it to complete the sentence.

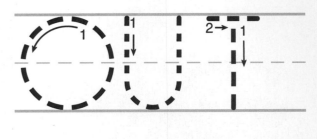

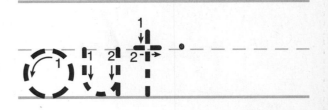

The bird is _____ of the nest.

out   out   out

Color the boxes with the word **out**.

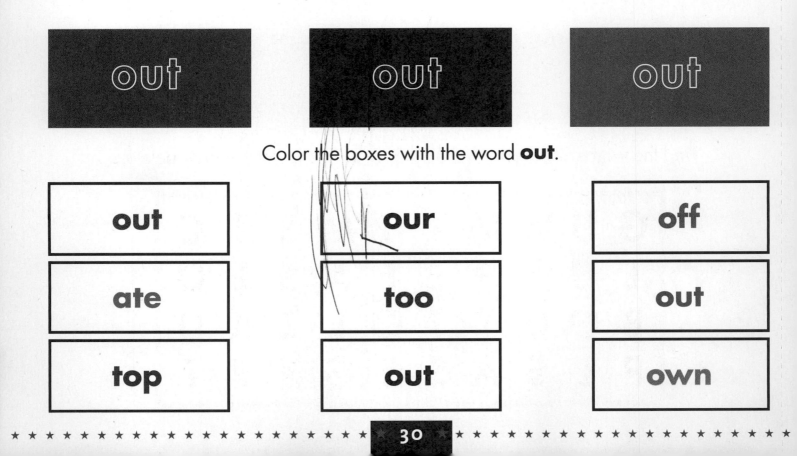

out	our	off
ate	too	out
top	out	own

Trace the sight word on the dotted lines. Write it to complete the sentence.

P_____ **come to my party.**

Find the words **OUT** and **PLEASE** 2 times in the word search below.

G U W M T I M S T C
L E F P L E A S E O
B O U T I Q L Z K U
P L E A S E G X P T

Done!

Places in my Neighborhood

A **neighborhood** is an area of a town or city where people live. Besides many different types of homes, there are a lot of different businesses there too. Look at each place and then circle the object that goes with it.

People in my Neighborhood

There are many helpful people in your **neighborhood**.
Match the helpers below with the object. Circle the correct answer.

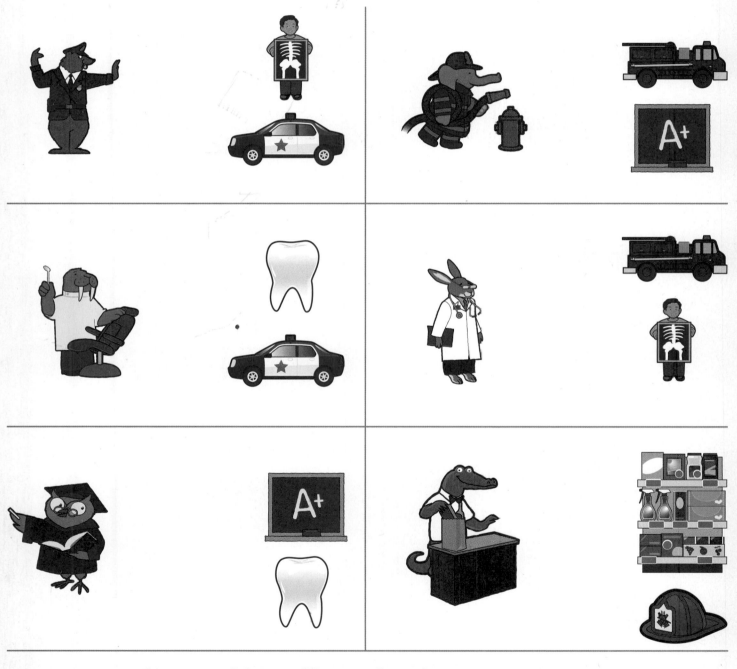

What would you like to do when you grow up?

Done!

Qq Rr Ss

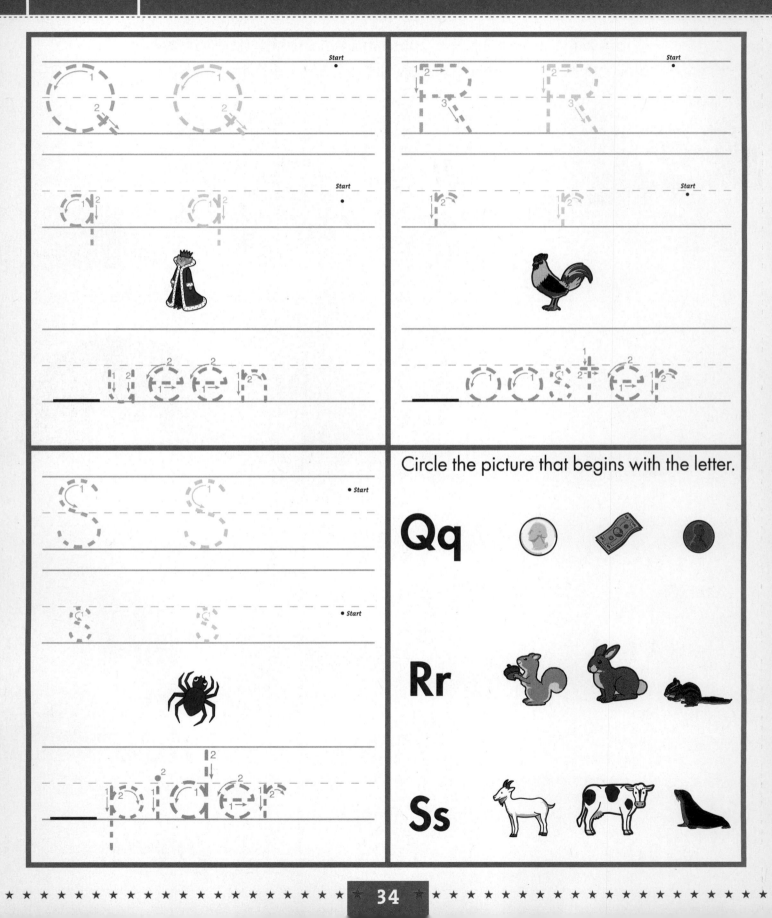

Circle the picture that begins with the letter.

Qq

Rr

Ss

Help the kids get out of the rain and find the rainbow by following the path of **Qq**, **Rr**, and **Ss**.

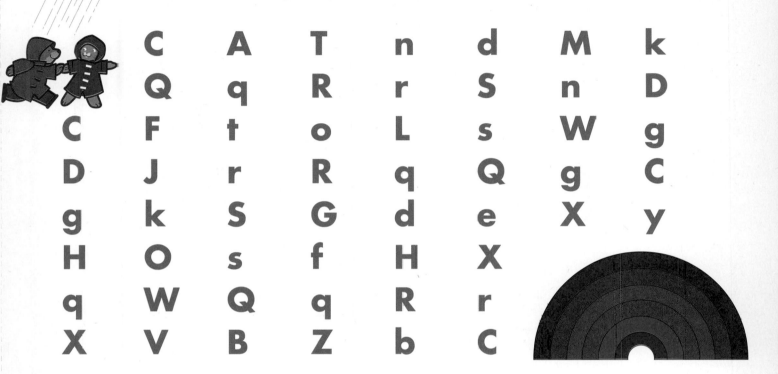

C	A	T	n	d	M	k
Q	q	R	r	S	n	D
C	F	t	o	L	s	W	g
D	J	r	R	q	Q	g	C
g	k	S	G	d	e	X	y
H	O	s	f	H	X
q	W	Q	q	R	r
X	V	B	Z	b	C

Circle the letter **r** in all the words below.

bear	rain	circle
red	three	there
run	purple	ride
four	are	green

SAY

Trace the sight word on the dotted lines. Write it to complete the sentence.

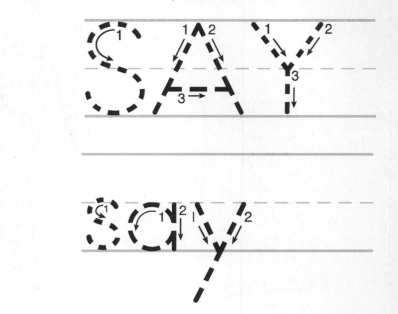

Let me _____ my name!

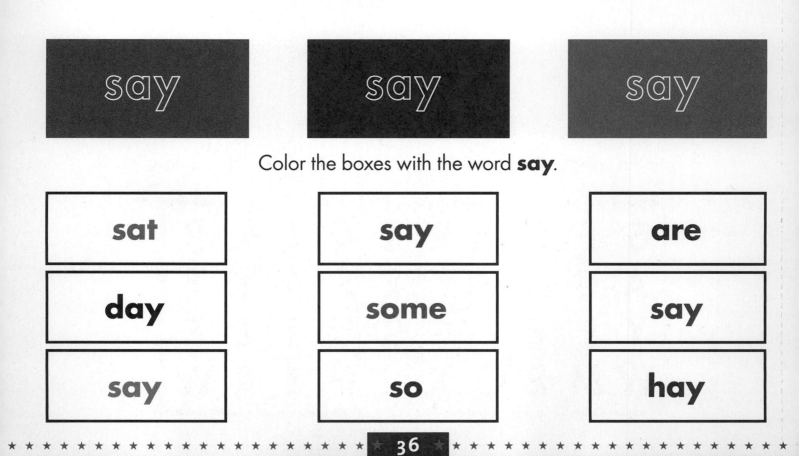

say   say   say

Color the boxes with the word **say**.

sat	say	are
day	some	say
say	so	hay

SHE

Trace the sight word on the dotted lines. Write it to complete the sentence.

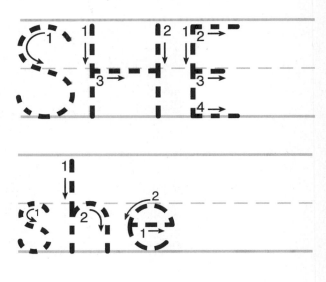

_____ **is my best friend.**

Find the words **SAY** and **SHE** 2 times in the word search below.

S	F	S	M	R	T	C	Z	K	P
A	U	H	H	X	E	S	A	Y	T
Y	E	E	L	G	K	U	I	L	F
W	M	E	G	X	S	H	E	R	W

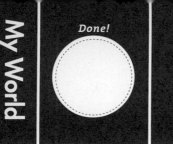

Animals and Their Babies

Draw a line from the parent to its baby animal.

House, Farm, or Zoo

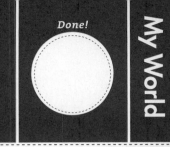

Draw a line from each animal to where you would find it;
in a house, on a farm, or in a zoo.

Done!

Tt Uu Vv

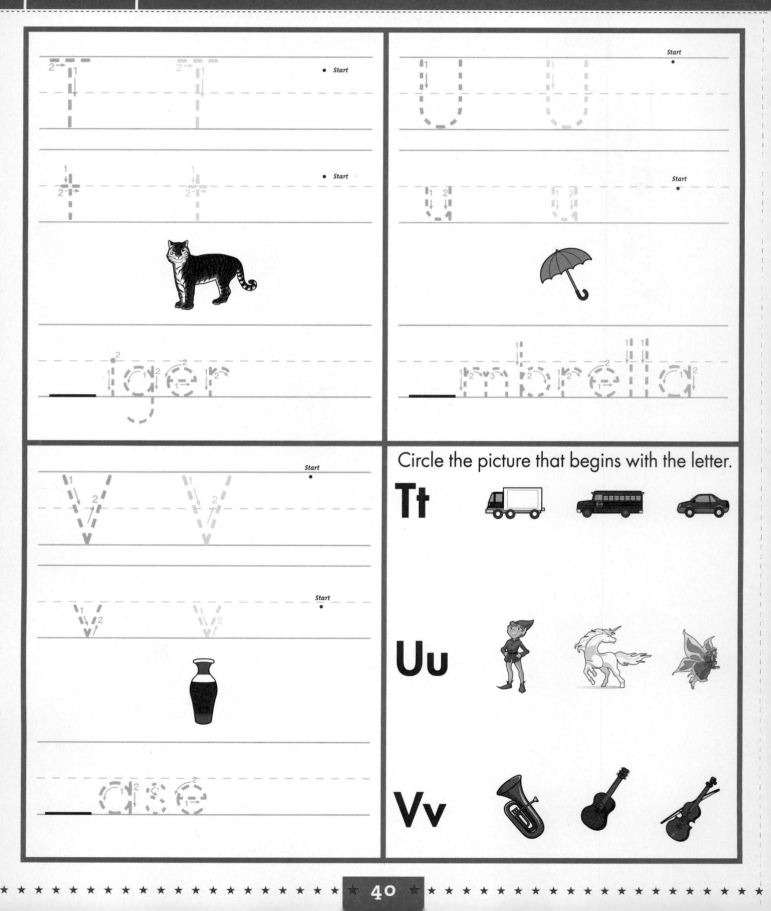

Circle the picture that begins with the letter.

Tt

Uu

Vv

Tt Uu Vv

Draw a line from the **UPPERCASE** letter to its matching **lowercase** letter.

Draw a line from the picture to the letter that begins the word. Then trace the letter.

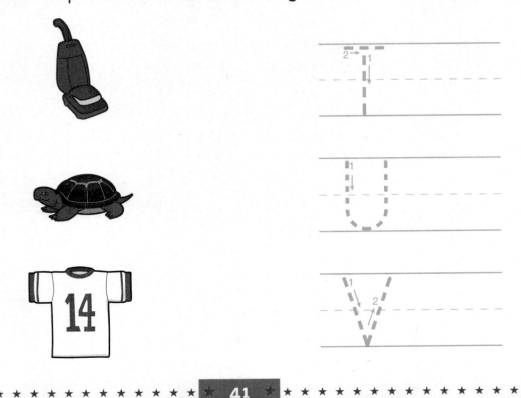

Done!

THEY

Trace the sight word on the dotted lines. Write it to complete the sentence.

Are _____ going to school?

Color the boxes with the word **they**.

they	that	them
there	they	this
this	the	they

Trace the sight word on the dotted lines. Write it to complete the sentence.

Is _____ chipmunk collecting acorns?

this   this   this

Find the words **THEY** and **THIS** 2 times in the word search below.

T	X	S	H	E	T	H	I	S	M
H	T	H	E	Y	P	H	U	E	H
E	E	B	A	Y	T	Y	I	Q	L
Y	K	T	H	I	S	W	M	S	G

Earth Day Every Day

Earth Day is on April 22 every year. Earth Day reminds us to take care of our planet by keeping it clean. Yet we should be doing that every day! We can do that with the idea of **reduce**, **reuse**, and **recycle**.

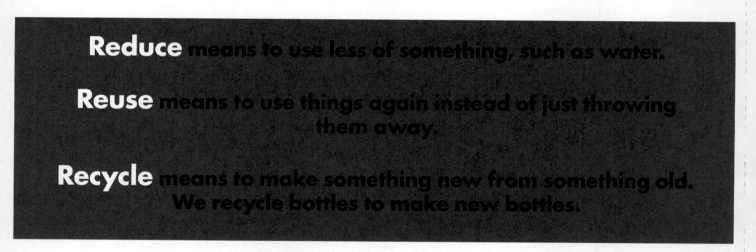

Reduce means to use less of something, such as water.

Reuse means to use things again instead of just throwing them away.

Recycle means to make something new from something old. We recycle bottles to make new bottles.

Look at the definitions above. Can you think of one example for each of how we can **reduce**, **reuse**, and **recycle**?

Color in the 3 **r**'s sign below. What color? **Green**, of course!

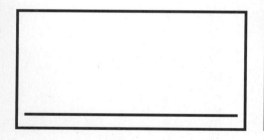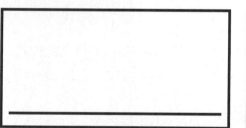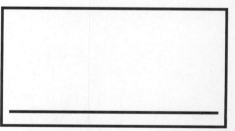

The 3 R's: Reduce, Reuse, and Recycle

Done!

Draw a line to help Mr. Can get to the correct bin in the recycling center.

CANS

Done!

Ww Xx Yy Zz

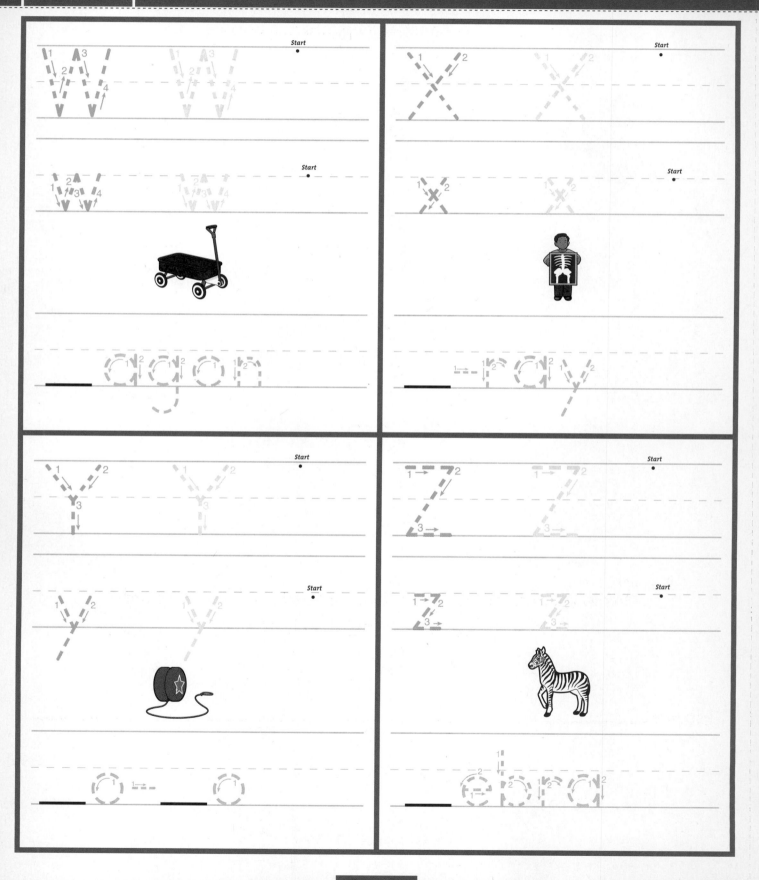

Ww Xx Yy Zz

Done!

Fill in the missing letters.

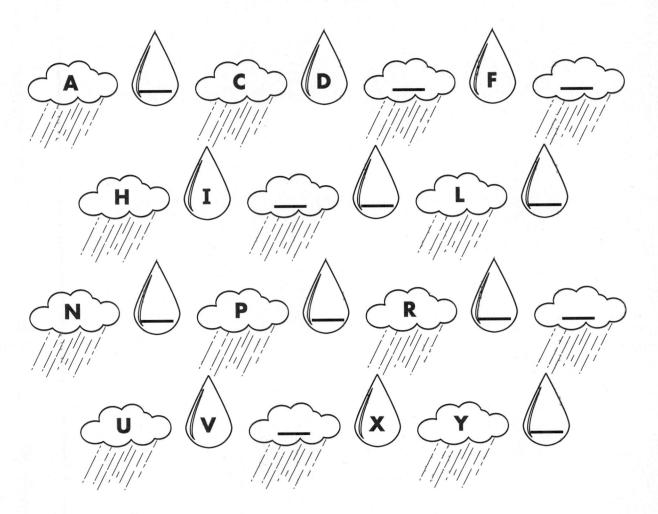

Write your first name on the line. Circle all the letters that are in your first name in the alphabet below.

Name _____

A B C D E F G H I J K L M

N O P Q R S T U V W X Y Z

ARE

Trace the sight word on the dotted lines. Write it to complete the sentence.

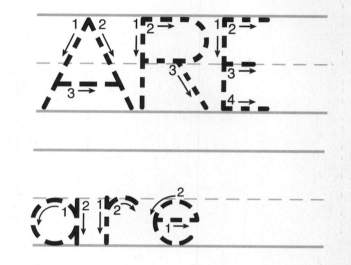

These spiders _____ **making a web.**

are   are   are

Color the stars with the word **are** in them.

are   art   am   and   or

ant   are   all   are

AT

Trace the sight word on the dotted lines. Write it to complete the sentence.

We met _____ the playground.

Circle the sight words **are** and **at** in the sentences below.

We are at the park.

Are you going to join us?

Meet us at 12:00.

Done!

All About Me

Draw a picture of **YOU** using the outline below. Look in the mirror first. What color hair and eyes do you have? Is your skin light or dark? Do you have short hair or long? When you're done, cut along the dotted lines and glue your drawing to a popsicle stick for a puppet of **YOU**!

All About Me

This Is Me

My name is ⎯⎯⎯⎯⎯⎯⎯⎯⎯⎯⎯⎯⎯⎯⎯⎯⎯⎯⎯•

I like to be called ⎯⎯⎯⎯⎯⎯⎯⎯⎯⎯⎯⎯⎯⎯⎯⎯•

My favorite food is ⎯⎯⎯⎯⎯⎯⎯⎯⎯⎯⎯⎯⎯⎯•

My favorite color is ⎯⎯⎯⎯⎯⎯⎯⎯⎯⎯⎯⎯⎯•

My favorite sport is ⎯⎯⎯⎯⎯⎯⎯⎯⎯⎯⎯⎯⎯•

My favorite book is ⎯⎯⎯⎯⎯⎯⎯⎯⎯⎯⎯⎯⎯•

My favorite animal is ⎯⎯⎯⎯⎯⎯⎯⎯⎯⎯⎯•

My favorite game is ⎯⎯⎯⎯⎯⎯⎯⎯⎯⎯⎯⎯•

Aa

1 2 1 2
3→   3→

Start

C C

Start

___corn

Bb

1 2 1 2
3   3

Start

1 1

Start

___at

Cc

1 1

Start

1 1

Start

___ar

Match the UPPERCASE letter
to its lowercase letter.

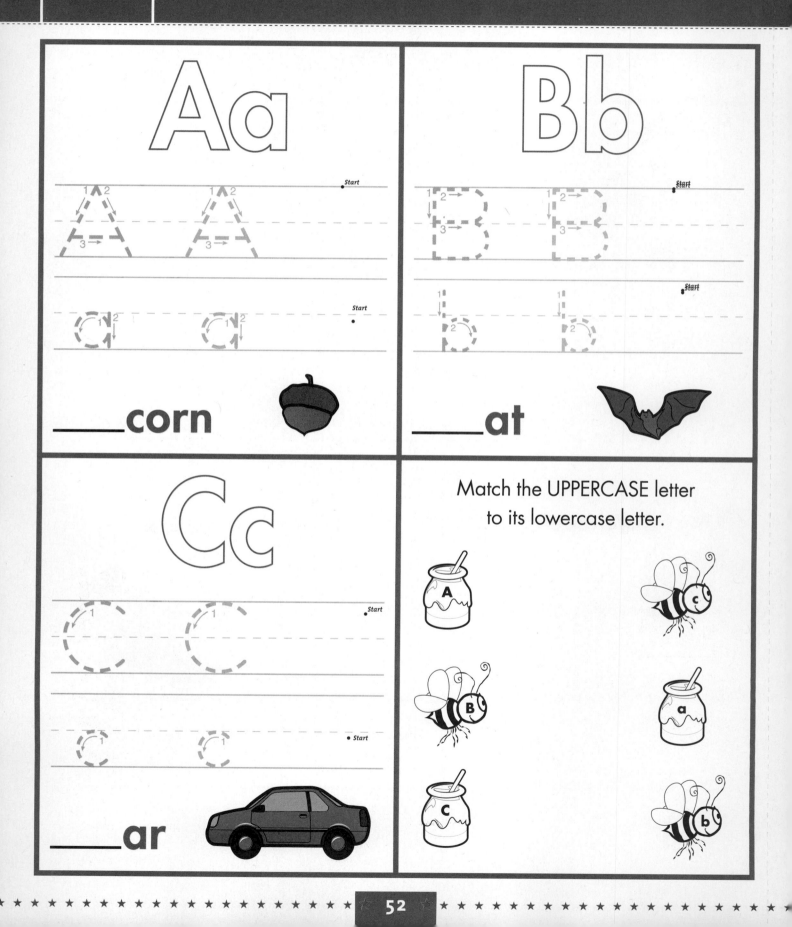

A

c

B

a

C

b

Circle the letter that is the beginning sound of the picture.

	a	B	c
	A	b	C
	a	B	c
	A	b	C
	a	B	c
	A	b	C

Draw a line from the UPPERCASE letter to its lowercase letter.

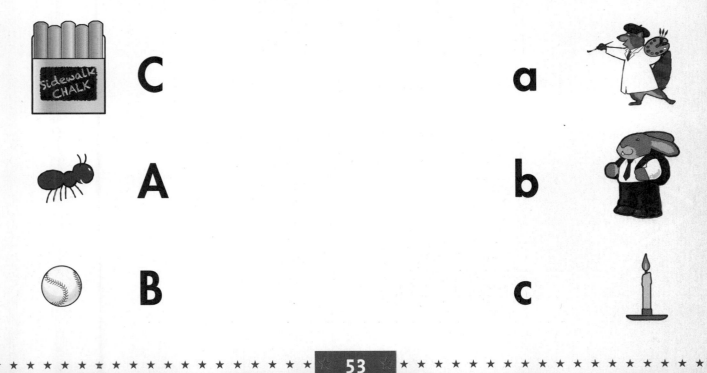

C   a

A   b

B   c

CAME

Trace the sight word on the dotted lines. Write it to complete the sentence.

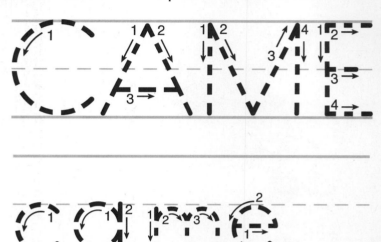

The kids _____ out to play in the rain.

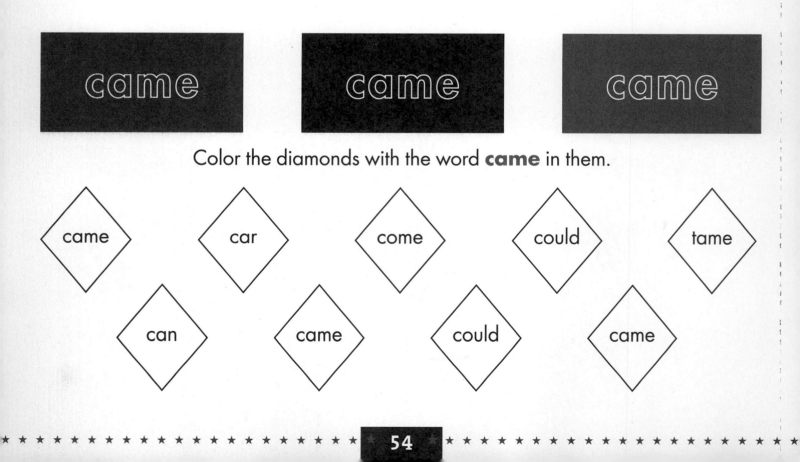

came   came   came

Color the diamonds with the word **came** in them.

came   car   come   could   tame

can   came   could   came

DO

Trace the sight word on the dotted lines. Write it to complete the sentence.

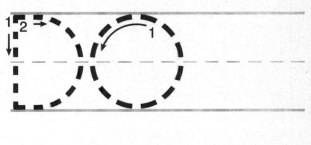

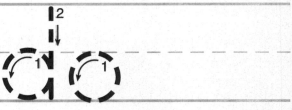

What sport _____ you like to play?

do   do   do

Circle the sight words **came** and **do** in the sentences below.

We came to play and have fun.

What do you like to do for fun?

Do you like to dance?

Done!

My Family Tree

This is a family tree. Draw a picture of yourself and your parents and then write your grandparents' names in. Cut out the tree and its base. Connect the two ends of the base with a sticker so that your family tree stands up. This is also something you could bring into class for show-and-tell or to tell the class a little something about you!

Family Traditions

A family tradition is something a family does together over and over that is meaningful to them.

Family traditions might be as simple as making the same peppermint cookies every Christmas, pizza night Fridays, or visiting the same cabin in Maine every summer.

Family traditions might have started years ago with your grandparents or started last month with your family.

Think about a **tradition** in your family. Draw a picture of it in the box below.

My Family Tradition

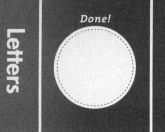

Done!

Dd Ee Ff

Dd

Start

____eer

Ee

Start

Start

____lf

Ff

Start

Start

____ire truck

Match the UPPERCASE letter
to its lowercase letter.

D

E

F

f

d

e

Dd Ee Ff

Color in the spaces with the letter **D green**, **E orange**, and **F yellow**
to see what begins with the letter **F**.

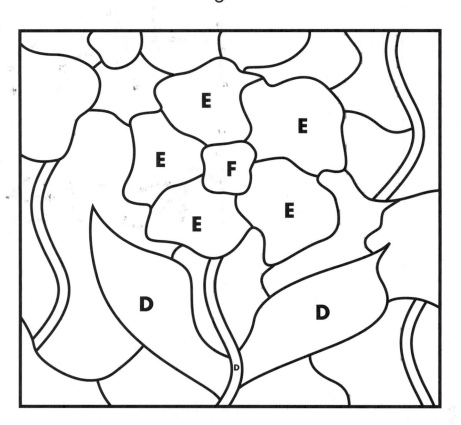

Circle the letters in each row that match the first letter.

D		D	B	D	A
d		b	d	d	p
E		F	E	E	B
e		e	c	e	o
F		F	T	P	F
f		p	f	t	f

Done!

HAVE

Trace the sight word on the dotted lines. Write it to complete the sentence.

I _____ a new kitten named Fluffy.

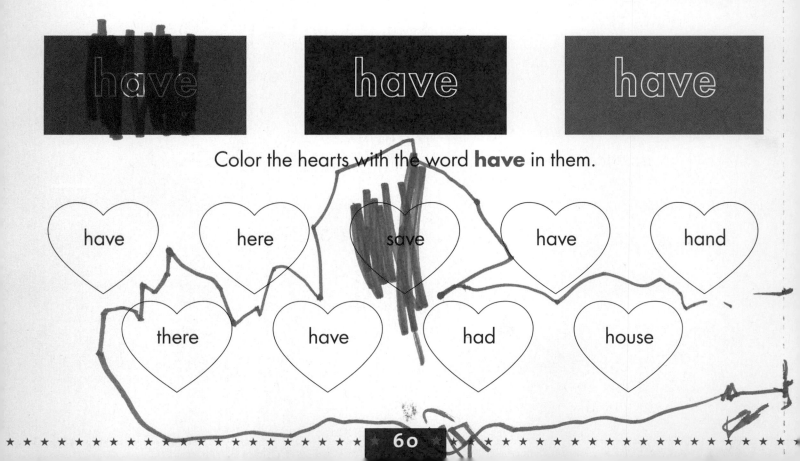

have   have   have

Color the hearts with the word **have** in them.

have   here   save   have   hand

there   have   had   house

HE

Trace the sight word on the dotted lines. Write it to complete the sentence.

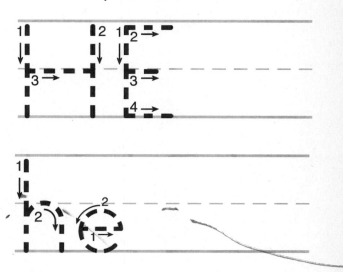

Is _____ your brother?

Circle the sight words **have** and **he** in the sentences below.

I have a little brother.

He is 3 years old.

He and I have a lot of fun together.

The Food Pyramid

This is a **Food Pyramid Plate**. It is used to help guide you toward eating the right amounts of healthy food every day.

Can you think of more foods in each food group?
Draw a picture of the food under the correct heading.

Fruits
_____

Grains
_____

Dairy
_____

Vegetables
_____

Proteins
_____

What Vegetable Am I?

It is important to eat your **vegetables** every day! **Vegetables** can add a rainbow of color to your meal, plus they keep you healthy!

Draw a line from the **vegetable** to its name. Color the **vegetables**.

tomato

carrot

corn

cucumber

peas

radish

potato

lettuce

Gg Hh Ii

Done!

Gg

Start

Start

___orilla

Hh

Start

Start

___eart

Ii

Start

Start

___ce cream

Match the UPPERCASE letter
to its lowercase letter.

G

H

I

i

g

h

Circle the picture that begins with the sound the letter makes.

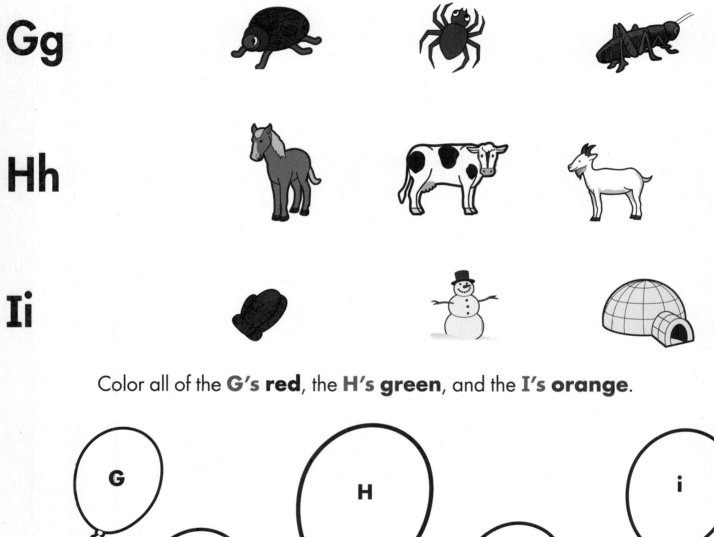

Gg

Hh

Ii

Color all of the **G's red**, the **H's green**, and the **I's orange**.

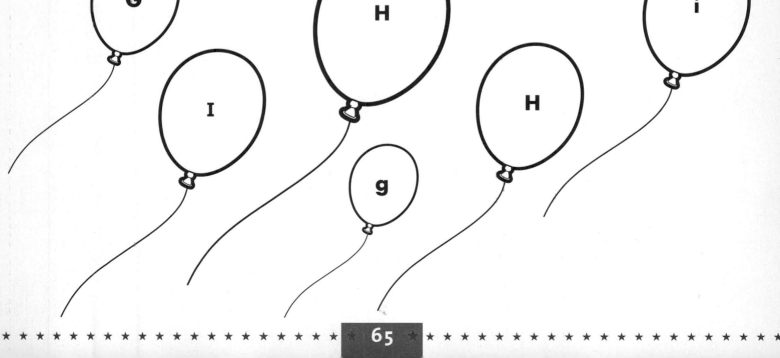

Done!

WILL

Trace the sight word on the dotted lines. Write it to complete the sentence.

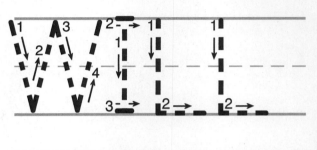

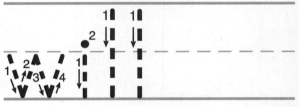

What animals _____ you see at the farm?

will   will   will

Color the circle with the word **will** in them.

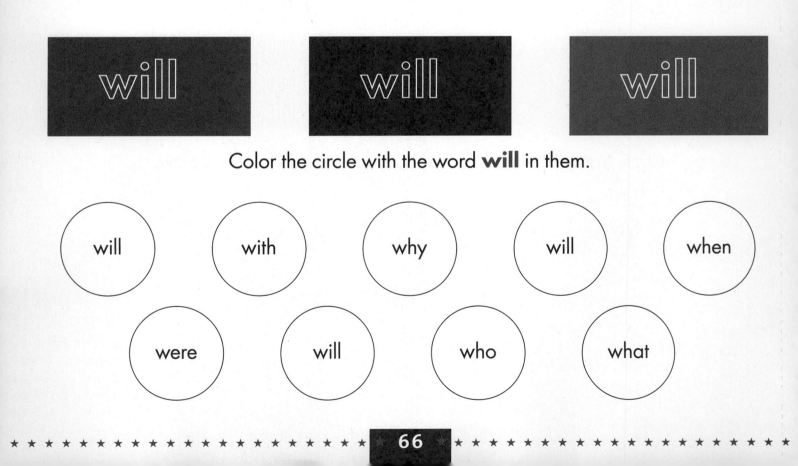

will   with   why   will   when

were   will   who   what

Trace the sight word on the dotted lines. Write it to complete the sentence.

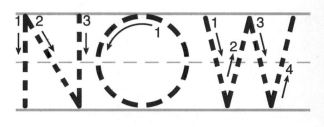

Please do your homework right _____.

Circle the sight words **will** and **now** in the sentences below.

Will you come here right now?

We will be leaving soon.

Now it is time to go.

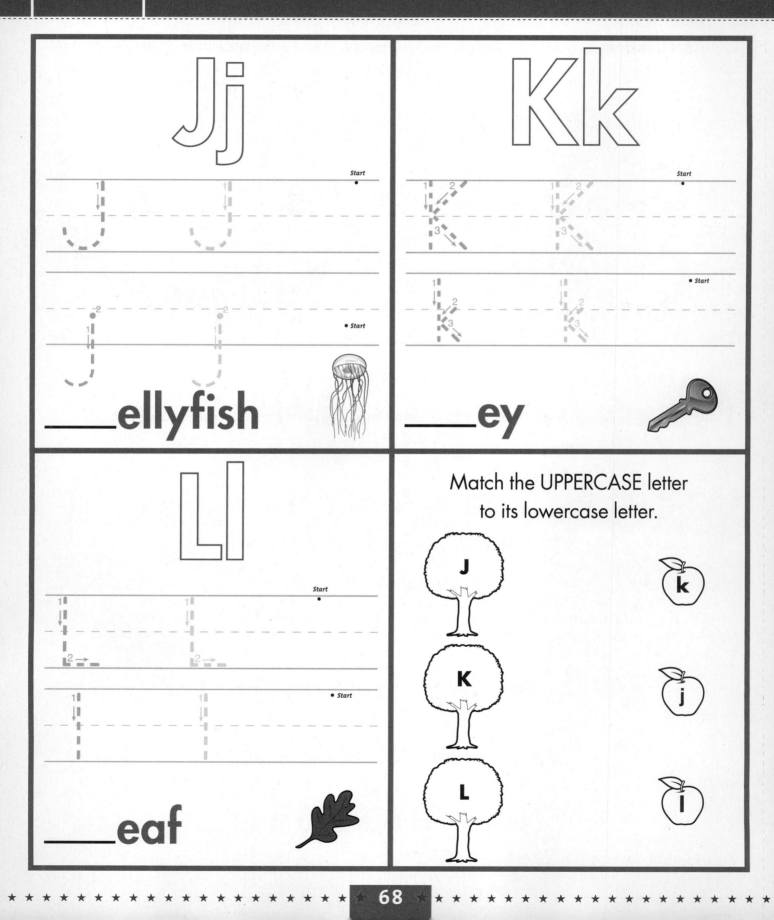

Jj

Start

____ellyfish

Kk

Start

Start

____ey

Ll

Start

Start

____eaf

Match the UPPERCASE letter
to its lowercase letter.

J

K

L

k

j

l

Jj Kk Ll

Done!

Connect the dots **a** through **l** in order to figure out the riddle below, then color it in.

I am big and round.

I have many faces.

I may be scary, but I have no guts.

What am I? I begin with the letter J.

Trace the word and then say it out loud. Listen to the sound **Ll** makes.
Now draw something that starts with the sound **Ll** makes.

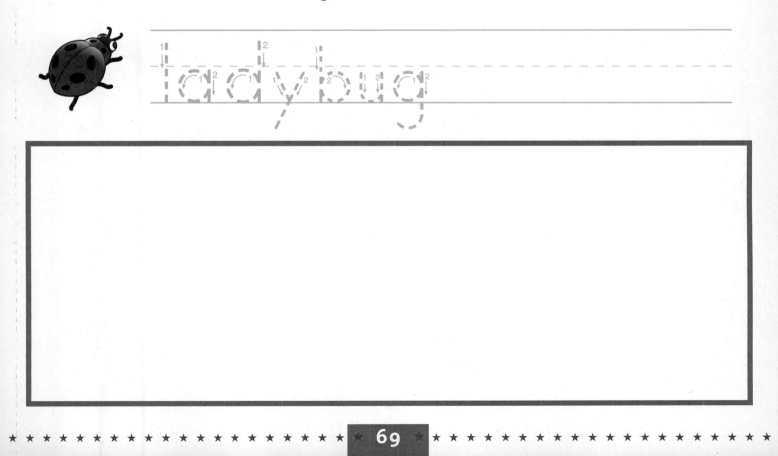

ladybug

PRETTY

Trace the sight word on the dotted lines. Write it to complete the sentence.

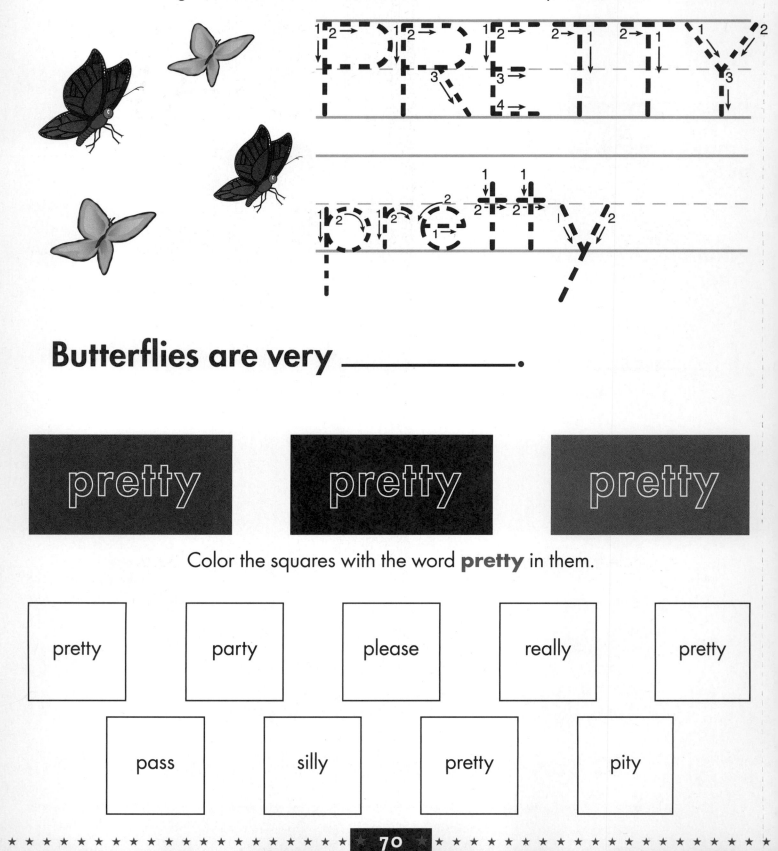

Butterflies are very _____.

pretty   pretty   pretty

Color the squares with the word **pretty** in them.

| pretty | party | please | really | pretty |

| pass | silly | pretty | pity |

Trace the sight word on the dotted lines. Write it to complete the sentence.

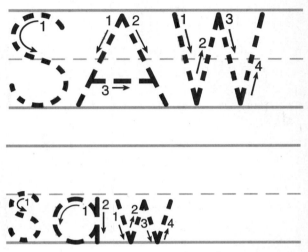

I _____ you at the park yesterday.

saw   saw   saw

Circle the sight words **pretty** and **saw** in the sentences below.

I saw a pretty ladybug sitting on a leaf.

It had six pretty spots.

When it saw me, it flew away.

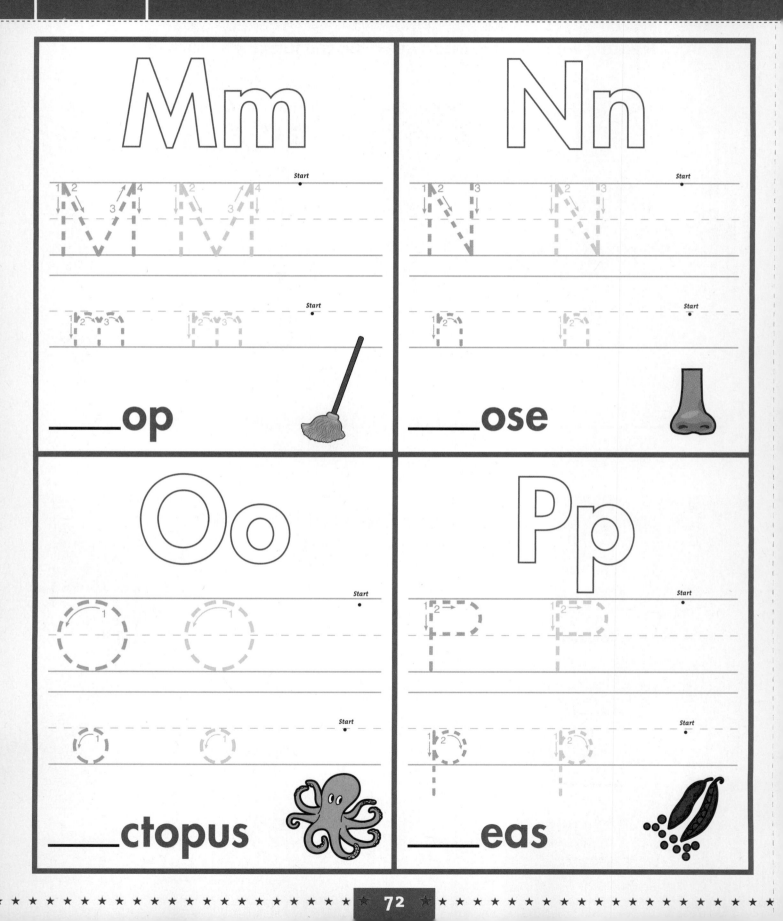

Mm

Start

___op

Nn

Start

___ose

Oo

Start

___ctopus

Pp

Start

___eas

Mm Nn Oo Pp

Circle the picture that begins with the sound the letter makes.

Mm

Nn

Oo

Pp

Look at the picture and write the missing letter that is the beginning sound.
Then draw a line to that letter.

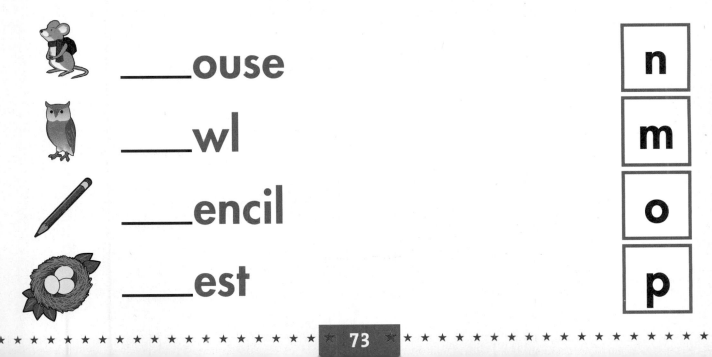

____ouse

____wl

____encil

____est

n

m

o

p

WHO

Trace the sight word on the dotted lines. Write it to complete the sentence.

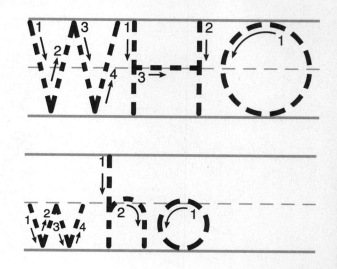

Guess _____ wants to skip rope?

who   who   who

Color the triangles with the word **who** in them.

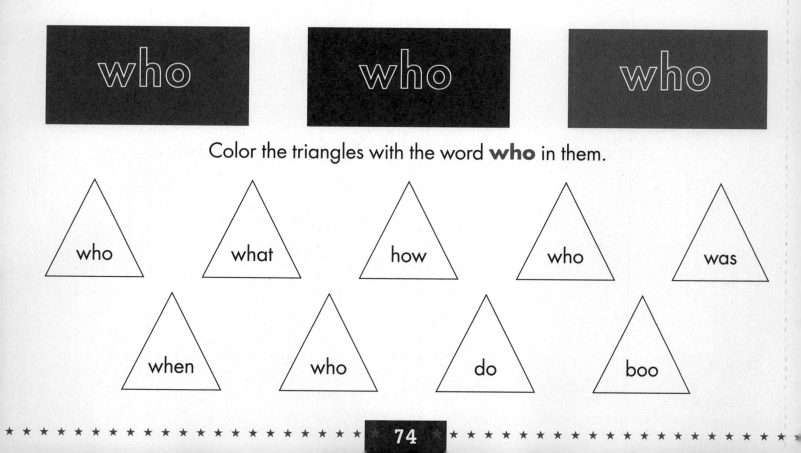

who   what   how   who   was

when   who   do   boo

Trace the sight word on the dotted lines. Write it to complete the sentence.

If I run, I will get there _____.

Circle the sight words **who** and **soon** in the sentences below.

Soon I will leave for camp.

I wonder who comes next.

Who will be in my cabin?

Qq

Start

____uarter

Rr

Start

Start

____ainbow

Ss

Start

Start

____eal

Match the UPPERCASE letter
to its lowercase letter.

Q   r

R   s

S   q

Qq Rr Ss

Help the seagulls get to the shore by following the path of **Qq**, **Rr**, and **Ss**.

Qq Rr Ss Qq Rr Ss Qq Dd
Mm Yy Bb Uu Mm Oo Rr Ll
Vv Hh Ss Rr Qq Ss Rr Qq Ss Yy
Uu Dd Qq Zz Ff Ee Oo Ii Nn Pp
Rr Cc Rr Oo Gg Pp
Tt Jj Ss Qq Rr Ss
Oo Pp m Bb Aa Ll

Circle the letter **s** in all the words below.

so	must	saw
she	say	soon
this	was	six
seven	sun	sat

Trace the sight word on the dotted lines. Write it to complete the sentence.

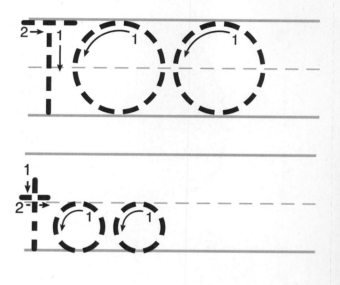

I play tennis and soccer, _____.

too   too   too

Color the stars with the word **too** in them.

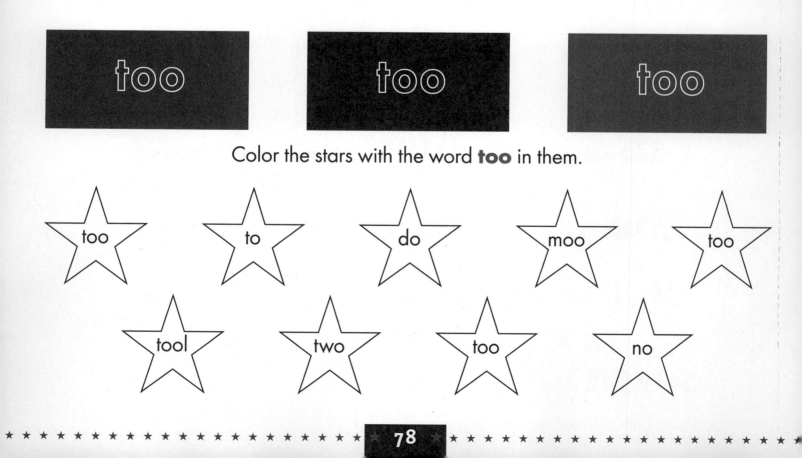

too   to   do   moo   too

tool   two   too   no

Trace the sight word on the dotted lines. Write it to complete the sentence.

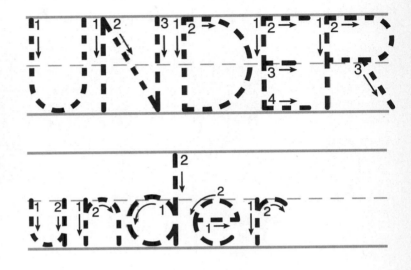

I like to sit _____ the tree.

under   under   under

Circle the sight words **too** and **under** in the sentences below.

I am standing under an umbrella.

My friend is under an umbrella, too.

We are both under an umbrella.

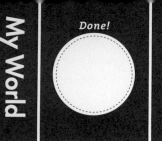
Reduce, Reuse, and Recycle

Reduce, Reuse, Recycle
(Sung to "Eensy Weensy Spider")

Reduce, Reuse, Recycle—words that we all know.

We have to save our planet so we can live and grow.

We might be only small children, but we will try, you'll see.

And we can save this planet—it starts with you and me!

Can you help sort the garbage?
Draw a line from each item to either a trash can or a recycling bin.

Reduce, Reuse, and Recycle

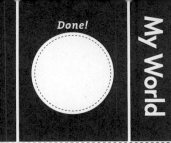
Done!

Look at the items below. Help recycle them by sorting them and drawing a line to the correct recycling bin.

PAPER

PLASTIC

CANS

Color in the earth below. Use **green** for the land and **blue** for the water.

Tt Uu Vv

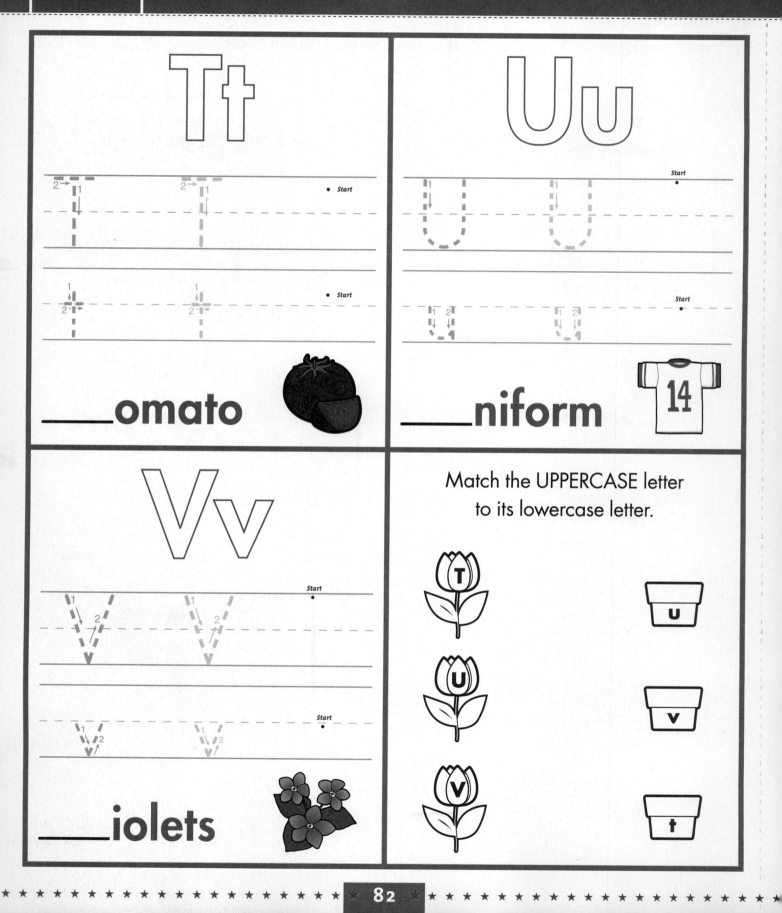

T t

Start

Start

___omato

U u

Start

Start

___niform

V v

Start

Start

___iolets

Match the UPPERCASE letter
to its lowercase letter.

T

U

V

U

V

t

Tt Uu Vv

Draw a line from the UPPERCASE letter to its matching lowercase letter.

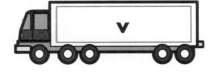

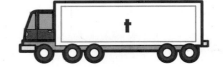

Draw a line from the picture to the letter that makes its beginning sound.

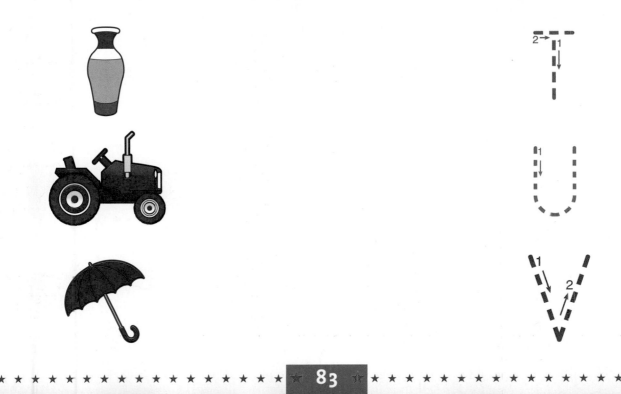

Done!

YES

Trace the sight word on the dotted lines. Write it to complete the sentence.

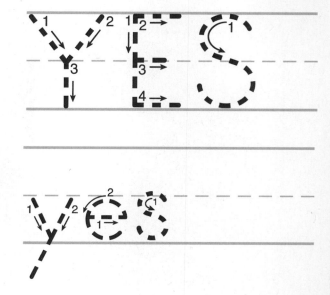

Y_____, I like to read!

yes   yes   yes

Color the word **yes**.

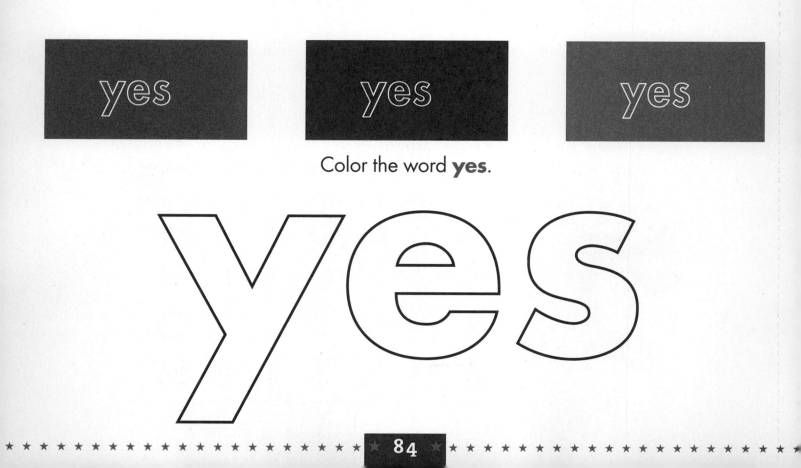

NO

Trace the sight word on the dotted lines. Write it to complete the sentence.

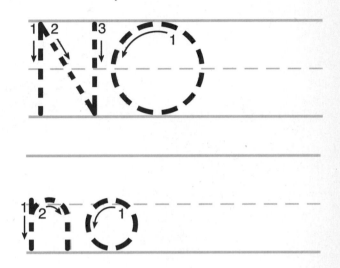

N_____, I do not like to go to the dentist.

no   no   no

Find the words **YES** and **NO** 2 times in the word search below.

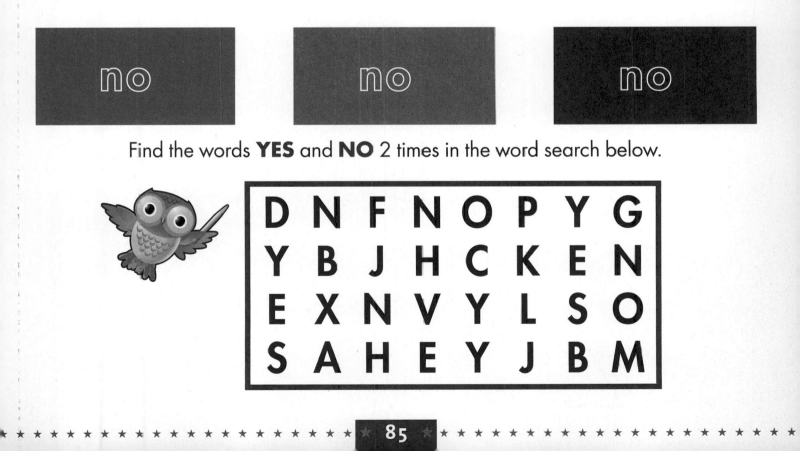

D N F N O P Y G
Y B J H C K E N
E X N V Y L S O
S A H E Y J B M

Ww Xx Yy Zz

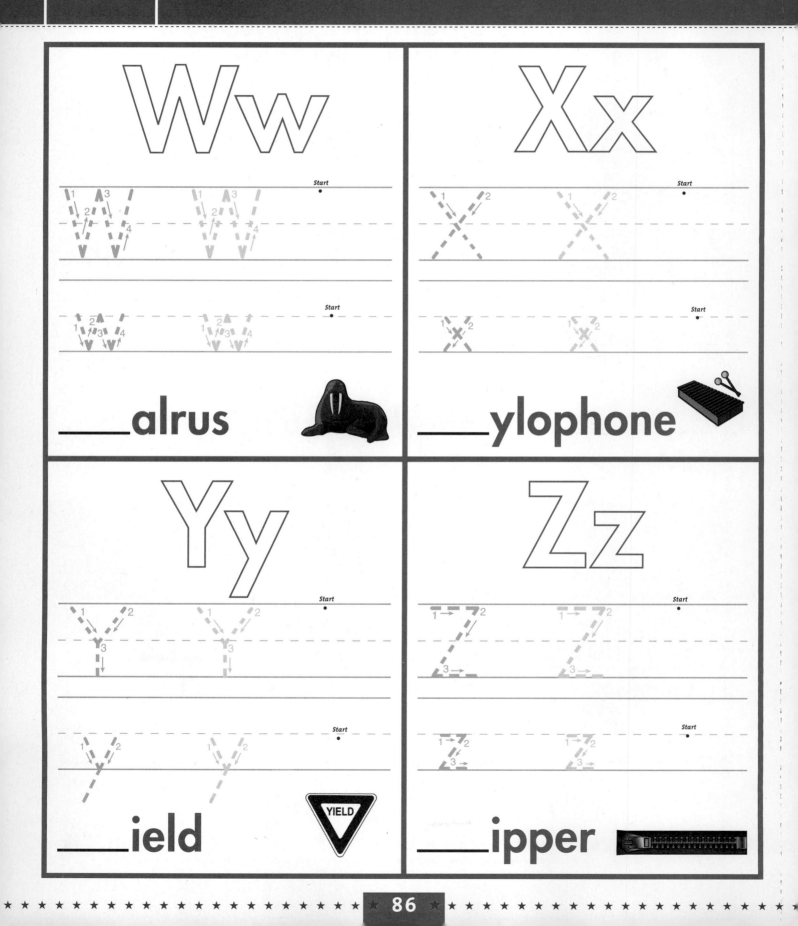

W w

Start

Start

___alrus

X x

Start

Start

___ylophone

Y y

Start

Start

___ield

YIELD

Z z

Start

Start

___ipper

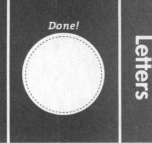

Done!

Fill in the missing letters.

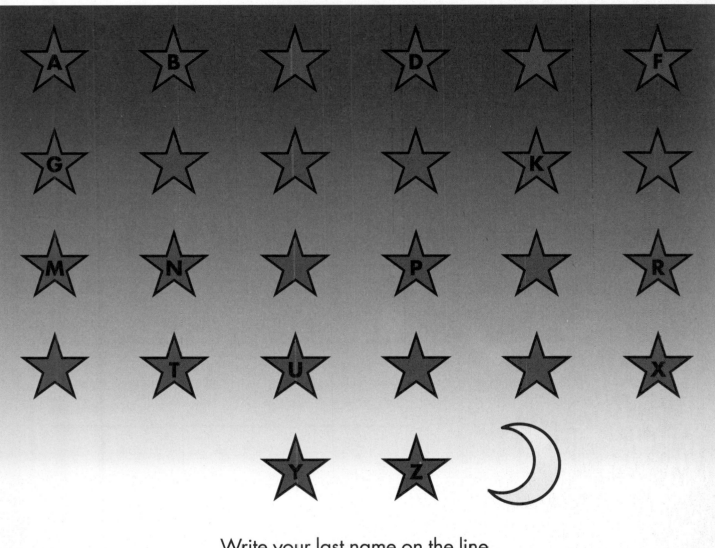

Write your last name on the line.
Circle all the letters that are in your last name in the alphabet below.

Name _____

A B C D E F G H I J K L
N O P Q R S T U V W X Y Z

Done!

All about Me!

Fill out all of the information below about YOU and then cut it out along the dotted lines. You or your parents can glue it to a piece of construction paper and you can keep it in your backpack. That way you will always have all your information on you!

My Name _____

My Street Address _____

My City or Town _____

My State _____

My Country _____

My Phone Number _____

Hand Print Bird

In the space below, trace your left and right hand with your fingers spread far apart. Cut out both hands and then use the bird sticker shown in the picture to tape together both thumbs. Then fold below the finger and tape the "wings" together.

Done!

Aa Bb Cc

____pple

____all

____amel

Aa Bb Cc

Circle the picture that begins with the sound the letter makes.

Aa

Bb

Cc

Draw a line from the UPPERCASE letter to its lowercase letter.

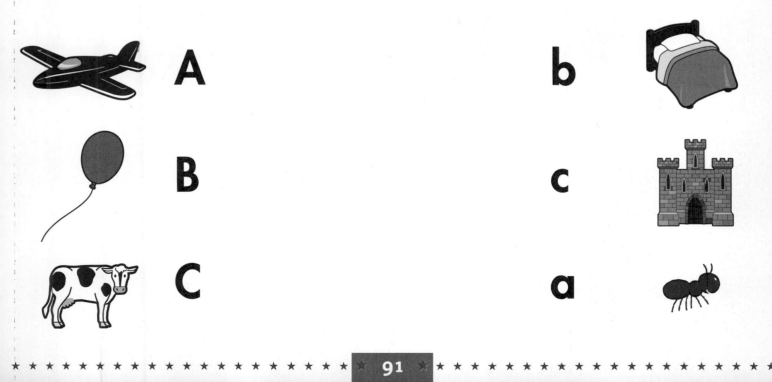

A

B

C

b

c

a

EAT

Trace the sight word on the dotted lines. Write it to complete the sentence.

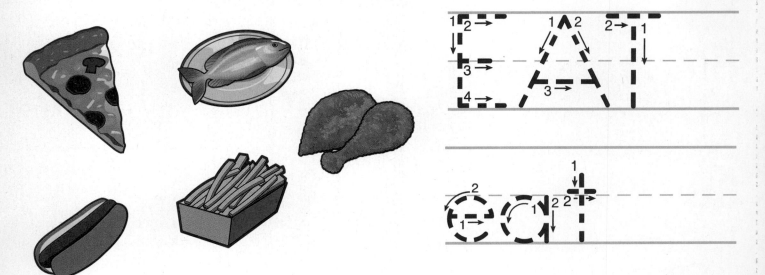

What is your favorite thing to _____ for dinner?

Color the word **eat**.

WENT

Trace the sight word on the dotted lines. Write it to complete the sentence.

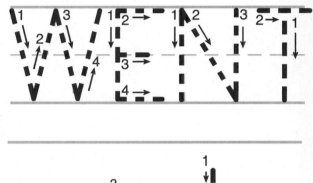

We _____ to the park to feed the ducks.

went   went   went

Find the words **EAT** and **WENT** 2 times in the word search below.

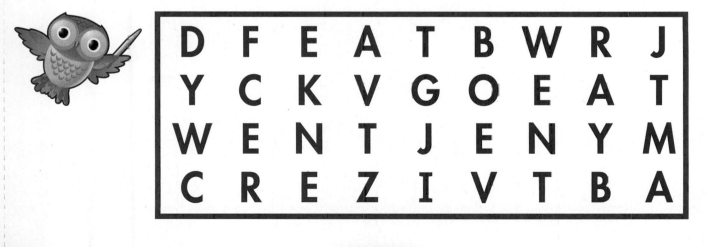

D	F	E	A	T	B	W	R	J
Y	C	K	V	G	O	E	A	T
W	E	N	T	J	E	N	Y	M
C	R	E	Z	I	V	T	B	A

Done!

Family Word Search

Look at the words listed at the top of the page. Find and circle them in the word search below. The words can be up, down, or across.

| brother | mom | grandma | sister | dad |
| aunt | cousin | grandpa | uncle |

```
h  c  a  t  t  t  d  a  d  r  e  r  r
b  r  o  t  h  e  r  a  g  l  a
w  x  o  o  u  d  o  s  r  y  u
c  t  w  t  w  a  k  o  a  s  n
o  s  v  b  h  y  h  h  n  i  t
u  u  m  s  u  e  u  i  d  s  u
s  m  o  m  g  e  r  b  p  t  z
i  t  n  x  u  l  h  g  a  e  b
n  u  n  c  l  e  j  y  v  r  v
h  a  v  d  t  c  e  f  d  g  e
d  u  g  r  a  n  d  m  a  v  r
```

Look at each picture and fill in the missing letters to spell the name of each family member correctly. Then try writing it yourself using words from the previous page.

m___m

d___d

s___ste___

br___the___

g___and___a

___ran___pa

Dd Ee Ff

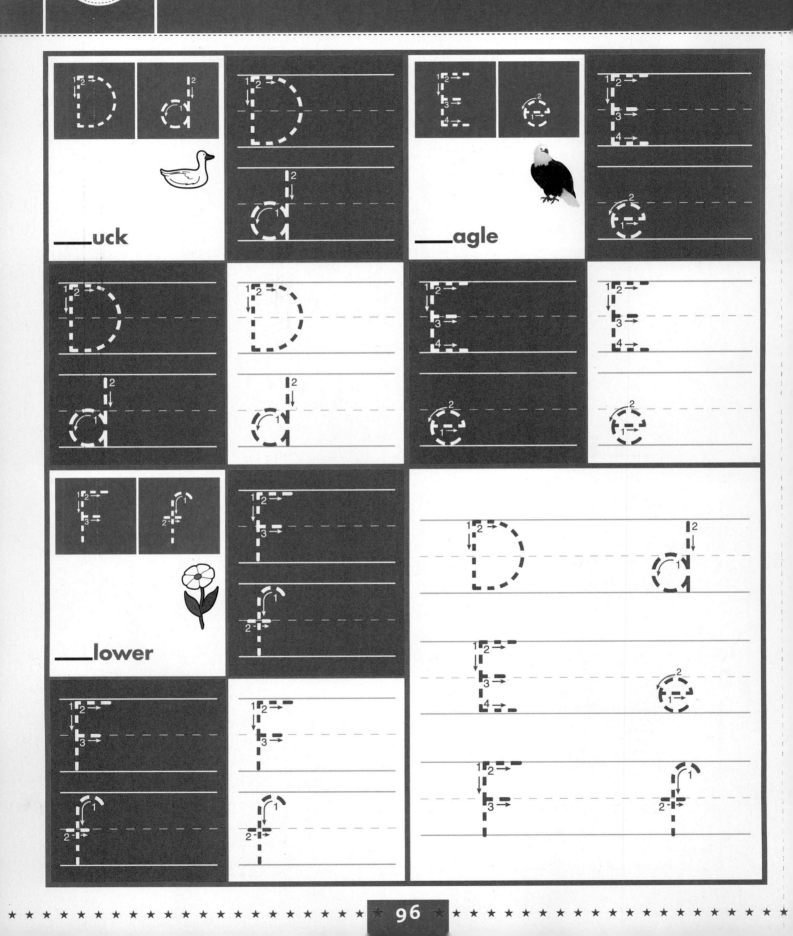

____uck

____agle

____lower

What animal can go for two months without water?
Connect the dots from **a** to **f** in order to find out.

Circle the letter in each row that is the beginning sound of the picture to the left.

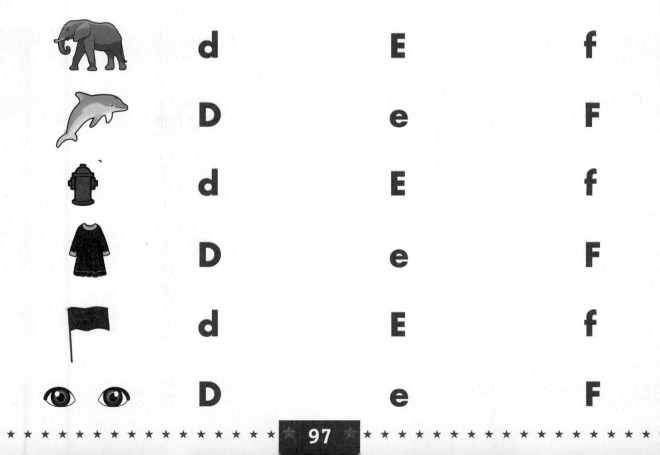

	d	E	f
	D	e	F
	d	E	f
	D	e	F
	d	E	f
	D	e	F

Trace the sight word on the dotted lines. Write it to complete the sentence.

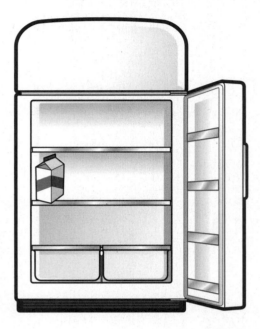 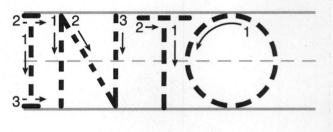

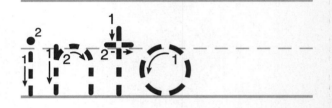

I put the milk _____ the refrigerator.

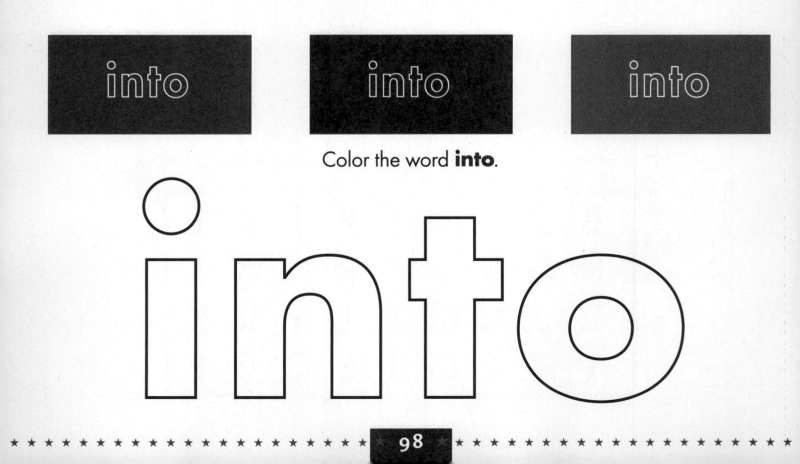

into into into

Color the word **into**.

into

LIKE

Done!

Trace the sight word on the dotted lines. Write it to complete the sentence.

Do you _____ to pop bubbles?

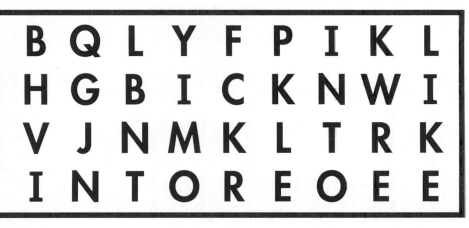

Find the words **INTO** and **LIKE** 2 times in the word search below.

```
B Q L Y F P I K L
H G B I C K N W I
V J N M K L T R K
I N T O R E O E E
```

Exercise is Fun!

Exercise is fun and keeps you healthy! **Exercise** helps strengthen your bones and muscles and keeps your heart healthy. There are many ways to **exercise** that are fun as long as you keep active or moving! Look at the pictures below.

Circle **active** or **not active** under each picture.

Active   Not Active

Active   Not Active

Active   Not Active

Active   Not Active

Active   Not Active

Active   Not Active

Active   Not Active

Active   Not Active

A Happy Heart

Done!

Eating well and exercising keeps your heart healthy and happy!
Draw a line from the activities below to either the happy and healthy
heart or the sad and tired heart.

Running around at the playground

Watching TV for hours

Dancing with a friend

Sitting on the couch

Taking a hike

Eating junk food

**Sitting in front of the
computer for hours**

Walking to school

Sleeping less than 8 hours a night

Skipping breakfast

Riding your bike

Drinking a lot of soda

Playing a game of tag

Gg Hh Ii

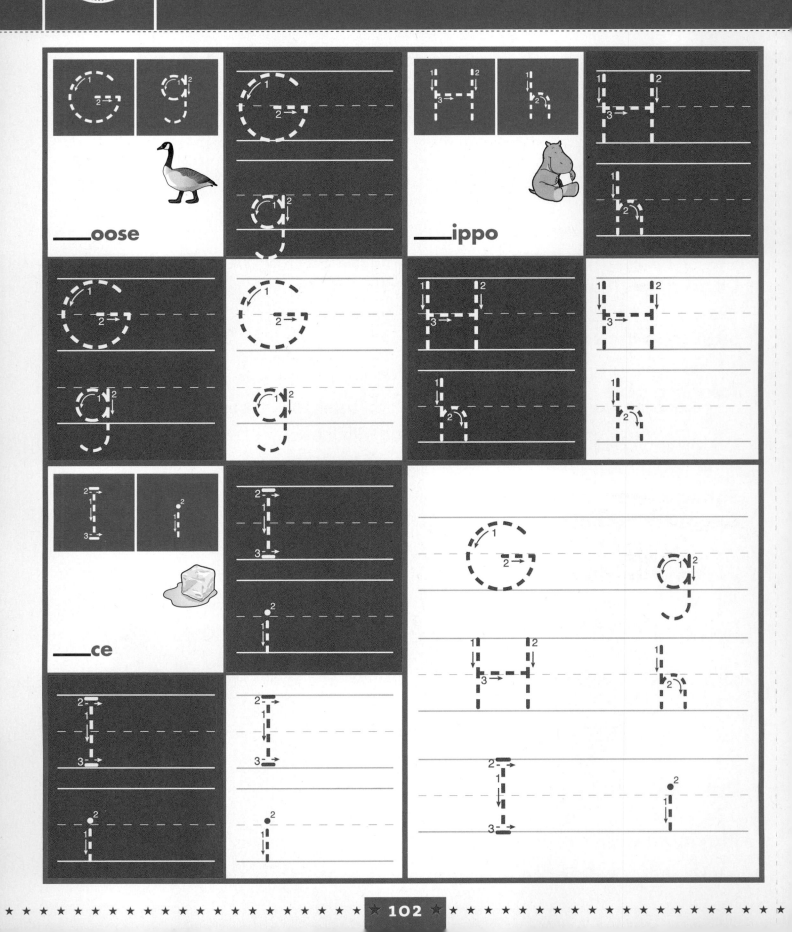

____oose

____ippo

____ce

Color all of the **G's red**, the **H's green**, and the **I's orange**.

Trace the word and then say it out loud. Listen to the sound **Hh** makes.
Now draw something that starts with the sound **Hh** makes.

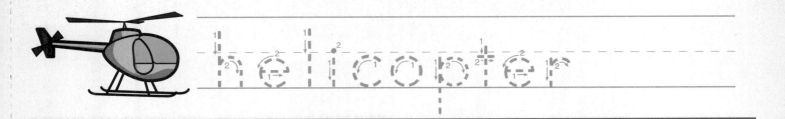

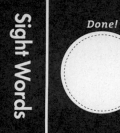
ON

Trace the sight word on the dotted lines. Write it to complete the sentence.

The bird landed _____ the tree.

on   on   on

Color the word **on**.

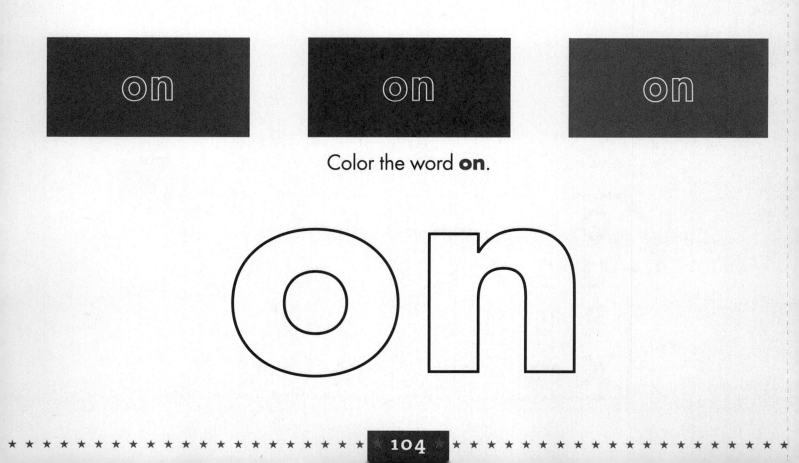

Trace the sight word on the dotted lines. Write it to complete the sentence.

This is _____ house.

our   our   our

Find the words **ON** and **OUR** 2 times in the word search below.

O H A O N K Y W Z
U C P H R L O N F
R B R J T E K R L
K N T D S M O U R

Done!

Jj Kk Ll

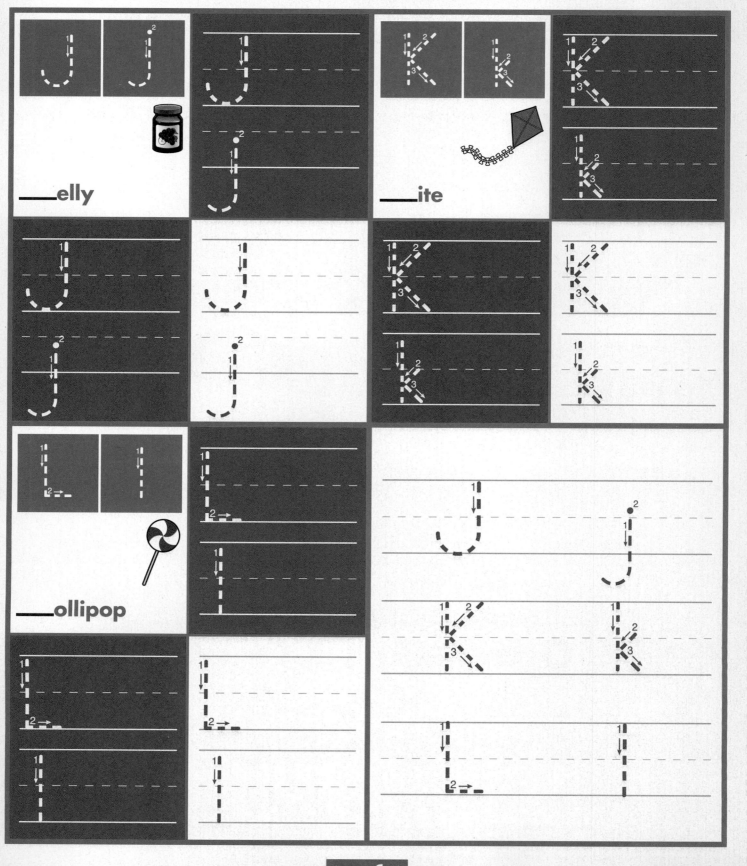

_____elly

_____ite

_____ollipop

Circle the picture that begins with the sound the letter makes.

Jj

Kk

Ll

Connect the dots **a** though **l** in order to find out which animal is the king of the jungle. Then color in the picture.

RIDE

Trace the sight word on the dotted lines. Write it to complete the sentence.

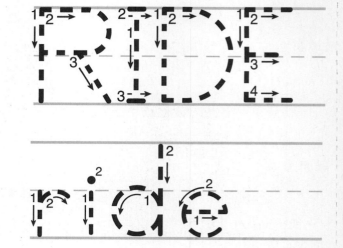

I know how to _____ a scooter.

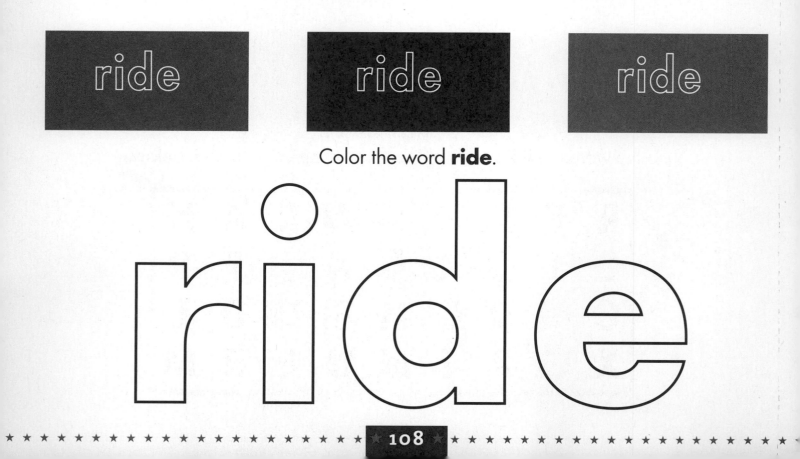

ride   ride   ride

Color the word **ride**.

RAN

Trace the sight word on the dotted lines. Write it to complete the sentence.

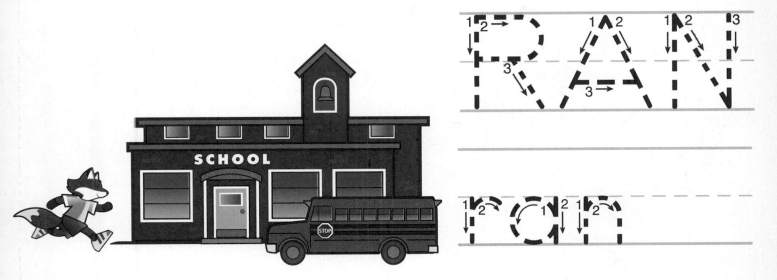

I _____ all the way to school.

Find the words **RIDE** and **RAN** 2 times in the word search below.

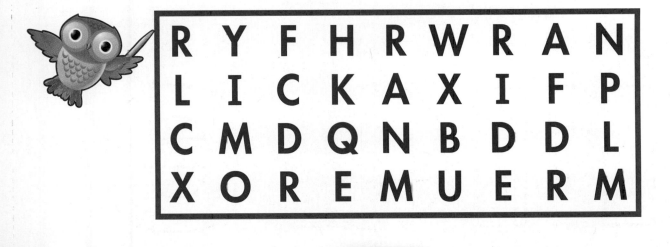

R Y F H R W R A N
L I C K A X I F P
C M D Q N B D D L
X O R E M U E R M

Mm Nn Oo Pp

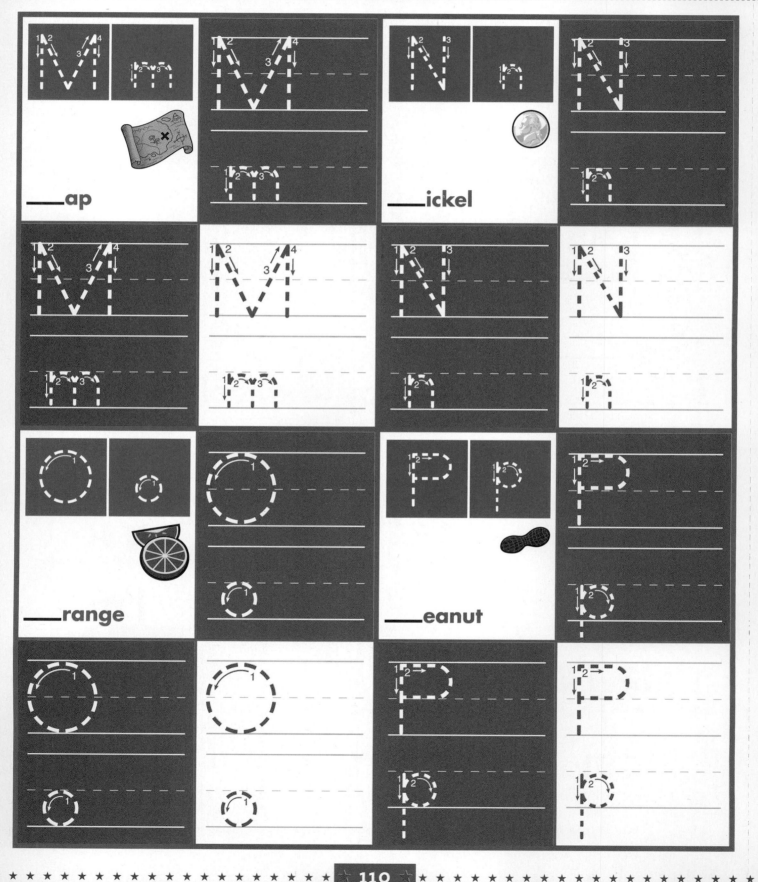

___ap

___ickel

___range

___eanut

Look at the picture and then write the missing letter that is the beginning sound. Then draw a line to that letter.

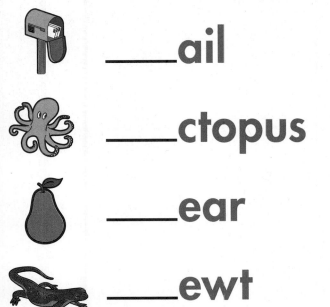

___ail

___ctopus

___ear

___ewt

| n |

| m |

| o |

| p |

Circle the letter **Mm** in all the words below.

mat   must   am

Monday   Sam   I'm

mad   moon   meat

Mom   arm   clam

THAT

Trace the sight word on the dotted lines. Write it to complete the sentence.

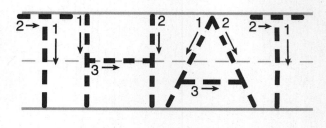

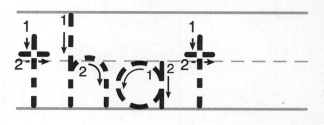

Did you enjoy _____ birthday party?

that   that   that

Color the word **that**.

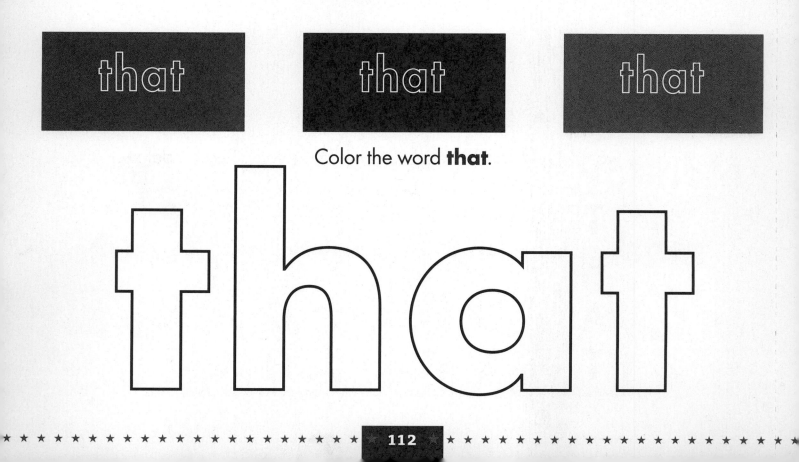

THERE

Done!

Trace the sight word on the dotted lines. Write it to complete the sentence.

T_____ are four chicks.

there   there   there

Find the words **THAT** and **THERE** 2 times in the word search below.

T Q L Y T H E R E
H G B I C K W N W
A J N M K L Q B N
T H E R E T H A T

Feathers, Fur, or Scales?

All animals have special traits that make them different from one another such as having feathers, fur, or scales.
Put the animals in the group where they belong.

Draw a square ⬛ **around all animals with feathers.**

Draw a circle ⬤ **around all animals with scales.**

Draw a triangle ▲ **around all animals with fur.**

Draw a line from the sound to the animal that makes that sound.

Baaaa

Mooo

Ribbit

Quack

Oink

Woof

Cock-a-doodle-doo

Qq Rr Ss

___uilt

___ooster

___cooter

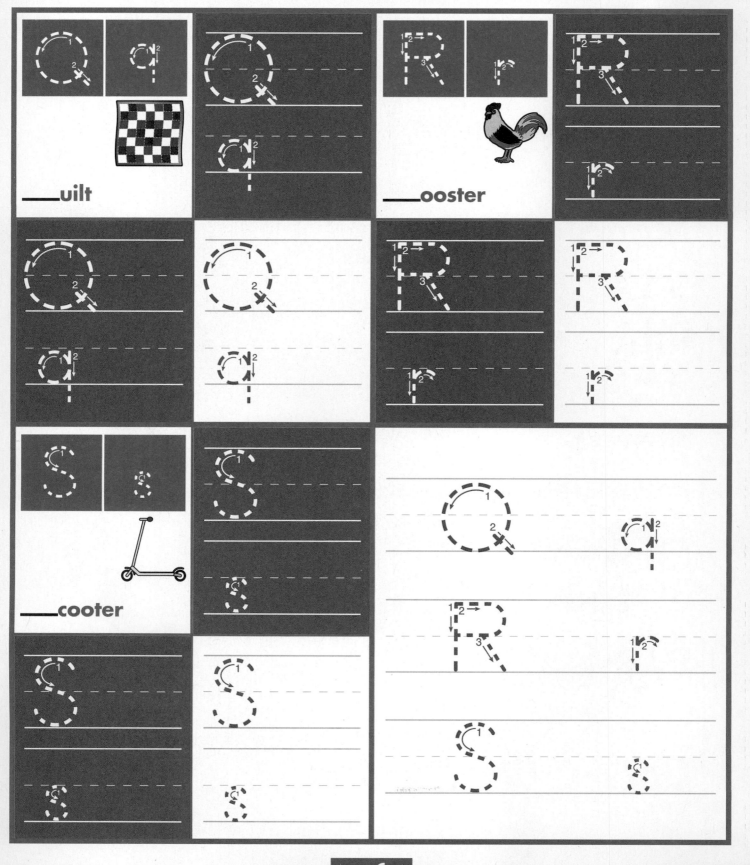

Qq Rr Ss

Draw a line from the UPPERCASE letter to its matching lowercase letter. Color in.

 Q

 r

 R

 s

 S

 q

Draw a line from the picture to the letter that makes its beginning sound.
Then trace the letter.

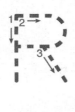

Trace the sight word on the dotted lines. Write it to complete the sentence.

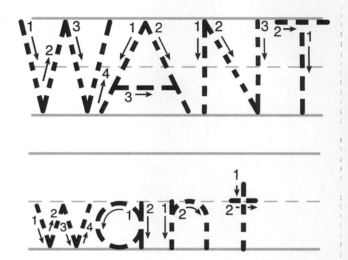

Do you _____ to go on the Ferris Wheel?

want   want   want

Color the word **want**.

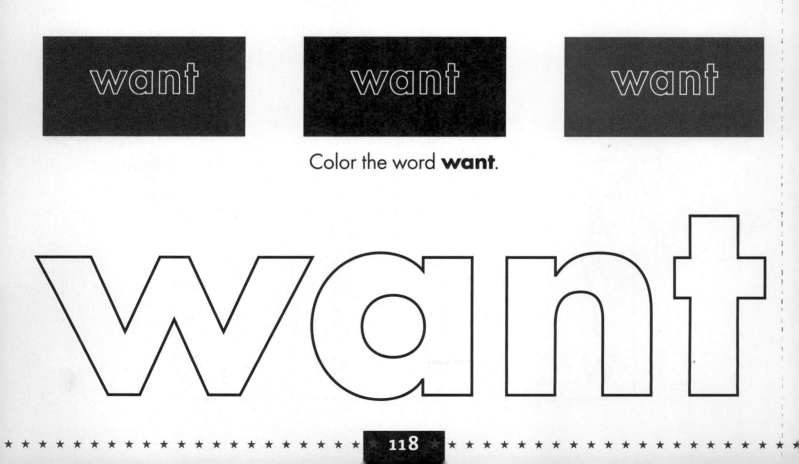

WAS

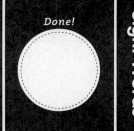
Done!

Trace the sight word on the dotted lines. Write it to complete the sentence.

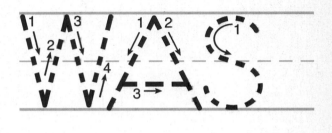

The butterfly _____ once a caterpillar.

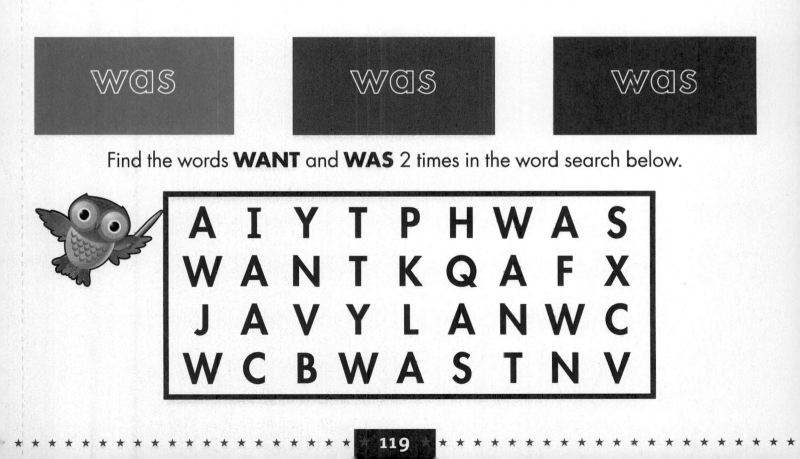

was   was   was

Find the words **WANT** and **WAS** 2 times in the word search below.

A	I	Y	T	P	H	W	A	S
W	A	N	T	K	Q	A	F	X
J	A	V	Y	L	A	N	W	C
W	C	B	W	A	S	T	N	V

____oad

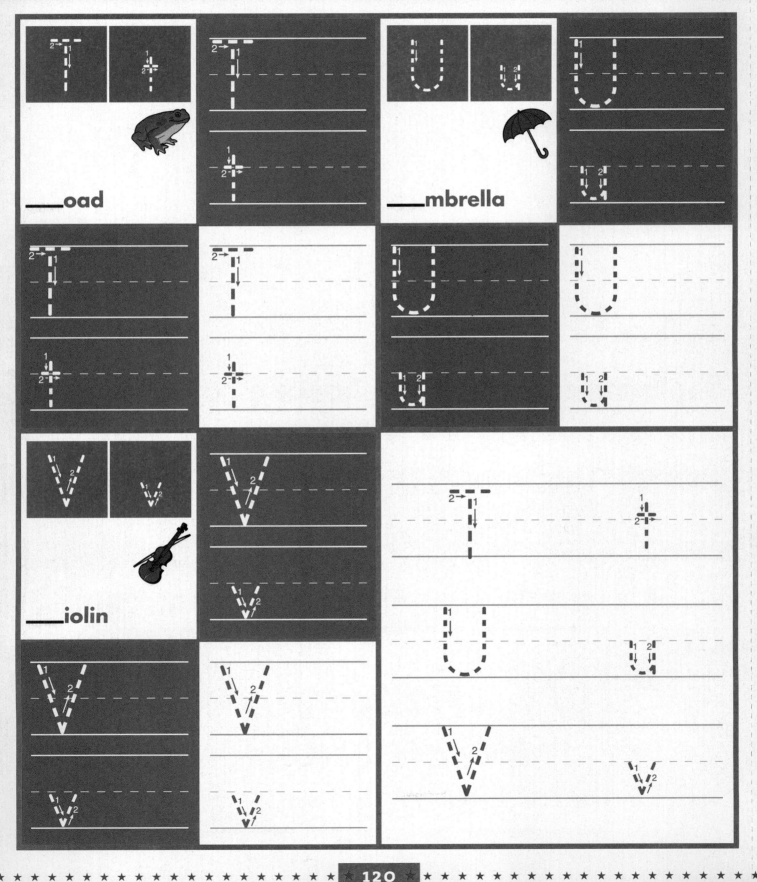

____mbrella

____iolin

Tt Uu Vv

Help the farmer find his tractor by following the path of **T**, **U**, and **V**.

Circle the letters in each row that match the first letter.

T		L	T	I	T
t		t	I	i	t
U		U	W	U	O
U		V	U	W	U
V		V	U	V	W
v		U	V	W	V

Done!

Places in My Neighborhood

A **neighborhood** is an area of a town or city where people live. Besides many different types of homes, many different places are found in a **neighborhood**, too.

Draw a line from each place on the left to the object that goes with it on the right.

People in My Neighborhood

There are many helpful people in your **neighborhood**. See if you can fill in the blanks below using the words from the word bank.

police officer	**doctor**	dentist	teacher	**grocer**	fire fighter

If I see something on fire, I can call a _____.

If I am in trouble and need help, I can call a _____.

If I need help learning how to read and write, I can go to my

_____.

If I need to buy food, I can go to my _____.

If I want to take good care of my teeth, I can go to see a

_____.

If I get hurt, I can go and see a _____.

What is your dad's job?

_____

Done!

Ww Xx Yy Zz

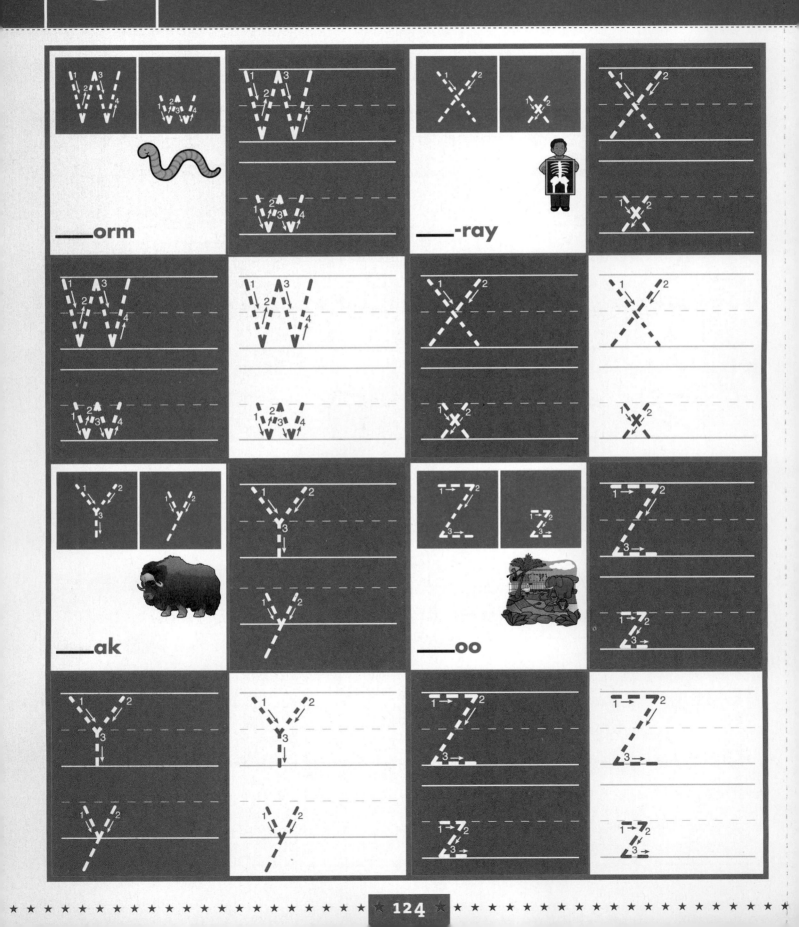

___orm

___-ray

___ak

___oo

Ww Xx Yy Zz

Fill in the missing letters.

Write the name of the town where you live.
Circle all the letters that are in your town in the alphabet below.

Name _____

A B C D E F G H I J K L
N O P Q R S T U V W X Y Z

Page 4 — Aa Bb Cc

Page 11 — Dd Ee Ff

Page 20 — The Food Pyramid Plate
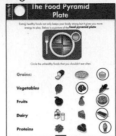

Page 29 — Mm Nn Oo Pp

Page 35 — Qq Rr Ss

Page 5 — Aa Bb Cc

Page 12 — BUT

Page 21 — Fruits and Vegetables

Page 30 — OUT
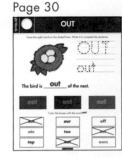

Page 36 — SAY

Page 6 — AM

Page 13 — DID

Page 22 — Jj Kk Ll
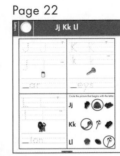

Page 31 — PLEASE

Page 37 — SHE

Page 7 — WITH

Page 16 — Gg Hh Ii

Page 23 — Jj Kk Ll
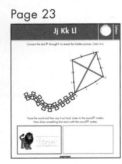

Page 32 — Places in my Neighborhood

Page 38 — Animals and Their Babies

Page 9 — Birthday Party Word Search

Page 18 — GET

Page 24 — MUST

Page 33 — People in my Neighborhood

Page 39 — House, Farm, or Zoo

Page 10 — Dd Ee Ff

Page 19 — GOOD

Page 25 — NEW

Page 34 — Qq Rr Ss

Page 40 — Tt Uu Vv

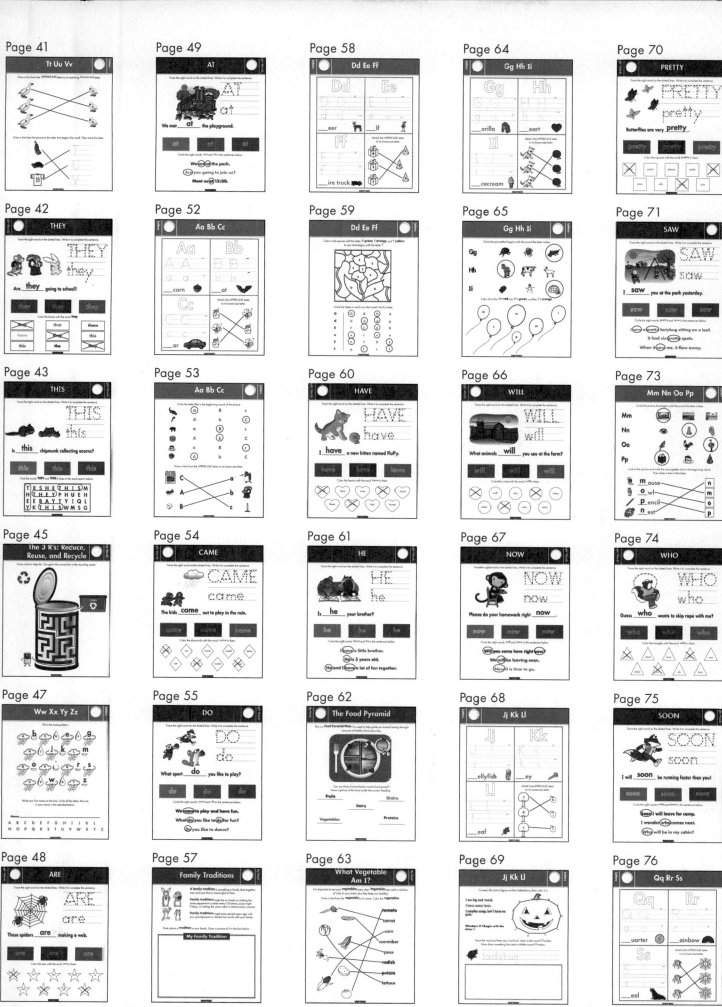

Page 77

Qq Rr Ss

Page 78

TOO

Page 79

UNDER

Page 80

Reduce, Reuse, and Recycle

Page 81

Reduce, Reuse, and Recycle

Page 82

Tt Uu Vv

Page 83

Tt Uu Vv

Page 85

NO

Page 87

Ww Xx Yy Zz

Page 91

Aa Bb Cc

Page 93

WENT

Page 94

Family Word Search

Page 95

Family Members Missing Letters

Page 97

Dd Ee Ff

Page 99

LIKE

Page 100

Exercise is Fun!

Page 101

A Happy Heart

Page 105

OUR

Page 107

Jj Kk Ll

Page 109

RAN

Page 111

Mm Nn Oo Pp

Page 113

THERE

Page 114

Feathers, Fur, or Scales?

Page 115

Who is Making That Noise?

Page 117

WAS

Page 121

Tt Uu Vv

Page 122

Places in My Neighborhood

Page 123

People in My Neighborhood

Page 125

Ww Xx Yy Zz